CULTURAL FELLOWSHIP OF BENGAL

CULTURAL FELLOWSHIP OF BENGAL

SISIR KUMAR MITRA

GYAN

Published by

Gyan Publishing House
5, Ansari Road
Daryaganj, New Delhi-110002
Phone: 011-47034999, 9811692060
E-mail: books@gyanbooks.com

Distribution Network
gyanbooks.com
India, USA, Canada, UK, Australia

ISBN: 978-93-7414-597-5 (PB)

First Published, 1946

2nd Impression 2025

Printed at: Gyan Press, Delhi.

CULTURAL FELLOWSHIP OF BENGAL
Author: SISIR KUMAR MITRA

CULTURAL FELLOWSHIP OF BENGAL

SISIRKUMAR MITRA

CALCUTTA
CULTURE PUBLISHERS
63, COLLEGE STREET

CONTENTS

ERRATA

Page	line	for	read
41	20	renaissance	resurgence
41	21	spirit	soul
74	10	is	gives
88	13	His	Him
92	5	comman	common

INTRODUCTION

A COMPREHENSIVE account of the cultural achievements of Bengal throughout the ages is yet a desideratum in Indian historical literature, since whatever treatment of the subject is available relates mainly to the march of political events in the country, in which adequate attention is scarcely given to the other equally, if not more, important expressions of Bengal's creative soul. It is unfortunate that many standard works on Indian history, too, should suffer fiom the same defect and be thereby responsible for spreading ideas about India which are largely inaccurate. That the spirit and forms of culture evolved in Bengal from very early times are not always properly appreciated is largely due to the paucity of authentic literature which can be called history in the deeper and wider sense of the term, revealing every aspect, no less than the significance, of the movements that took place in the inner and outer life of the people inhabiting that ancient land and mothered by her as 'the flesh of her flesh, the bone of her bone'.

There is no doubt that lack of reliable materials has sometimes made the historian's task apparently difficult, but he has very little to say against the charge that he has seldom troubled to tap and explore and make proper and systematic use of the sources that are available in the traditions and customs, religious and spiritual practices, in literature and in the folk-forms of culture, whose discovery would require a great deal of patient and continued investigation.

With the help of the glimpses so far afforded by recent researches into the past of Bengal an attempt is made in these essays to give some idea of the cultural fellowship that had started to grow in that country from very early days and continued throughout her history expressing itself in new and varied forms. It is remarkable that foreign invasions and other adverse conditions have not always proved unfavourable to the development in Bengal of a feeling of cultural confraternity among her different sects and communities through contacts mainly in the sphere of religion in which they seem to be so divergent to-day. Even if it be conceded that this feeling was only a beginning in its earlier phases, it must be admitted that it was a great beginning, not always the result of any conscious effort, but a free natural growth fostered by all the wealth of the Bengali heart.

Indeed, an inclination to join with others for the attainment of a common end is ingrained in the racial being of Bengal. And nowhere is it more marked than in her efforts to give form to her ideals in the domain of her spiritual culture: for, in her great days religion was to her not so much a body of rituals as a cult of inner practice, a way to regeneration into higher states. It is because of these tendencies of her soul that Bengal along with the rest of India, has been able to stand through the ages in order to fulfil her destiny in a greater future.

In a deeper sense the cultural fellowship of

Bengal is an ever-enlarging process of her cultural evolution. When sufficient light will be thrown on her early history, it will be found that a supine self-forgetful people inhabits that country to-day, innocent of a knowledge of its great past, of the romantic story of how its forebears had been helping all along through her varied religious and social endeavours to lay the foundation of a marvellous synthetic culture that might seem to be the goal towards which Bengal has been moving from the very dawn of her history. And her achievements in the recent past indicate the progress she has made in her path towards that goal.

Some of the facts and events showing the growth of Bengal's cultural fellowship from the early times to the present day are recounted in this brief survey intended for the general reader.

THE CULTS OF BENGAL

The Basis of Her Fellowship

It is generally held that her late Hinduisation is one of the chief reasons why Bengal has been able to acquire traits that distinguish her from the rest of India, giving her a stamp of individuality. Not a little of this, however, she owes to her love of freedom in the body politic. No doubt she cherished this love in common with many other States and kingdoms into which northern India of old was divided. But what marks her out is her genius to make bold experiments which she has been carrying on for centuries towards the building up of a synthetic culture. And among these the most remarkable have been her inward adventures which have resulted in the evolution of a number of esoteric cults of spiritual humanism which are peculiar to her spirit, and which attest her passion to discover the secret of life so that it might unfold itself as a field of mystical experiences whose flowering would lift the seeker into higher realisations. It is while engaged in these deeper quests that the seekers of Bengal were vouchsafed the vision of the truth of humanity and of its essential oneness in the world of the Spirit. They, therefore, felt urged from within to give more importance to the collective aspect of the spiritual life so that the progress towards the goal might also be a uniform social growth in the community life of the people.

The early schools of Upanishadic mysticism, the Tântric Chakras, the Buddhist Sanghas, the Vaishnavite Goshthis, and other similar circles or orders in Bengal were not bound by any rigid rules with regard to the admission of new entrants. Caste, creed, or birth was not to them the criterion of judging a man's spiritual seeking. They, therefore, each in its day, were open to all, the low as well as the high, the neophyte as well as the advanced, and their teachers were eager to help the true aspirant, the aim always being to spread the doctrines of their respective schools. Thus these centres of inner culture developed into meeting-places of men and women of all denominations who by their allegiance to a common ideal were united into a kind of spiritual brotherhood, which was almost a marvel in human relations, although its purity, especially where opposite sexes came into contact, could not, for obvious reasons, be maintained all through. It is true that these cults of Bengal had each its secret conclave, but its object was to preserve the basic truth—the seed Mantra—of its respective discipline, and that as nothing more than a nucleus round which the order would grow drawing its inspiration from it. They were not like the similar institutions of orthodox Hinduism running along parochial grooves.

to which admission was secured by birth or pedigree. It is not yet known what exactly was the extent of success that each of these schools achieved, but there is no gainsaying the fact that they effected a wonderful fusion of many castes and communities which *per se* might be taken as an important factor in the social and cultural progress of the people.

An abundance of emotion is a distinctive characteristic of Bengal. It has given her an unbounded ardour and warmth of the heart, an impassioned longing for the comradeship of others, not only in her cultural pursuits but also in her search for the ultimate truths of life. It is this emotional bent that has helped Bengal to develop a catholic outlook and inspired to a great extent her efforts to bring together men of all castes, creeds, and races under the banner of one religion, the religion of love, which is a true Dharma of her soul. And if to its excess might be traced one of the causes that were responsible for her failure to achieve all the high aims of her religious movements, it has to be acknowledged as having given Bengal that readiness and enthusiasm with which she broke into those movements and thereby promoted fellowship of a unique kind.

Mothered by her rivers, enriched by Nature with her boundless gifts, Bengal knows nothing so utterly as the infinite Mother in things. And it is to this cult of her soul, more than to anything else, that Bengal owes her almost inexhaustible creative energy whose glorious expressions illumine the pages of her history. Due to the vandalism of man and the ravages of time no less than those of the very rivers which are her chief source of sustenance, Bengal has lost much of her achievements in the past. And she has very little of them even in her memory. This might be a reason why tradition has never had any firm hold on her. Freedom to grow in her own way has ever been the insistent demand of her soul, so much so that she has developed a kind of reckless abandon that impels her to venture into the unexplored, to set out for the unknown. She is ever wide in her heart, ever open in her mind, freely receiving inspiration from others and making it her own by giving it a new turn. Thus whatever she evolves or creates always bears the stamp of her distinctive genius. And of these creations the most important to her evolution are those in the world of the spirit, through which Bengal in the past laid the foundation of her cultural fellowship.

The *Chhândogya Upanishad* speaks of a higher knowledge which was the exclusive possession of the Kshatriyas. It was from the Kshatriyas that the Brahmins obtained this knowledge. They taught the supreme necessity of self-culture even to the Brahmins. This esoteric philosophy had its origin in Mithila: it spread to Magadha but achieved a fuller development in Anga and Vanga

(Bengal). Thus the early Kshatriya mystics of Bengal were among the pioneers in evolving a new form of inner culture from the teachings of the Upanishads, and their success in that direction has yet to be properly assessed as one of the remarkable contributions of ancient Bengal in the domain of Indian thought. The object of this intrinsic spiritual endeavour was the truth that is realised in the soul and not mere knowledge that is acquired by the intellect for its own sake. Yet knowledge was not ignored, but was cultivated by them so that the mind might grow into an instrument of intuition, just as the emotions were heightened by them into intense aspiration that was at the back of all their inward seeking.

It is said that the cult of Bhakti, which thrives well in emotional natures, had been prevalent in India even in prehistoric times. That it was there at the time of the early Aryans is suggested by the Vedic hymns and the invocations addressed to various gods. But it took a more definite form in the later Upanishads in which was developed out of the Pranava ('Om') the philosophy of the Pancha-upâsanâ, or fivefold worship, *viz.*, the worship of Shiva, Devi, Sun, Ganesha, and Vishnu. These cults, based on devotion, began to spread all over India, and helped in absorbing into the Aryan fold new communities of men, the 'non-Vedic hordes and races', who were seen in India after the Kurukshetra War. The Vedic orthodoxy, confined within its religious formalism and social exclusiveness, was not only unequal to the task but was positively against the movement initiated by the liberal exponents of these schools with the object, among others, of quickening the process of Aryanisation that had begun long ago but could not make much progress owing to the obscurantism of the Vedic priests. The origin of the Tantras is traced to this fivefold worship. Bengal, emotional by nature, felt an instinctive leaning towards Tantric Sâdhanâ. And she gave her whole soul to it so as to be able soon to make an important contribution to the formulation of its doctrines, the worship of Shakti therein having appealed to her more than the other forms. Tantricism in Bengal, therefore, emphasizes a whole-hearted consecration to Mahâmâyâ as a fundamental principle of its practice. It is well known that over her long past Bengal has been a recognized seat of Tantric culture, and she is so deeply imbued with its spirit that she may be said to have received from it the very core of her spiritual being. For whatever might be her religious aspirations, in her inmost soul Bengal knows only one truth, the truth of the Supreme Shakti. But the Shakti does not awake in Her human vehicle unless and until its inmost heart, the centre of psychic emotions, opens to Her Light.

It is held that the Mahayana Buddhism as prevalent in Bengal was largely derived from the

Bengal school of Tantricism in which knowledge blended with devotion into a wonderful system of inner discipline that rose to heights scarcely attained by any other spiritual effort of mankind. Similarly, her devotional nature is one of the reasons why Bengal welcomed with all her heart the Mahayana form of Buddhism which upheld Bhakti and allowed the adoration of the personality of the Tathagata and various gods and goddesses. Bengal felt no attraction for the Hinayana, the orthodox path, which forbade these, and encouraged only an ethical idealism and ascetic denial of life. In the Mahayana path devotion and knowledge coalesced to make of it that popular religious cult which flourished so remarkably in the soil of Bengal owing mainly to its being fertilized by a flood of emotion. Yet there is much truth in the view that an excessive play of emotions was to a certain extent responsible for the corruptions that crept into both Tantricism and Buddhism. In their raw and unregenerate state, human emotions are either the splash and spatter of desires and passions that rage in the lower vital or a mere surface stir worked up by the mind in an access of sloppy sentimentality. When the emotional being is agitated, the intelligence gets clouded and the vital turbidity surges up and swamps the whole consciousness. The inevitable result is a lapse from true knowledge into an erotic or neurotic morbidity and a disintegrating excess. Thus fell Vaishnavism from the purity of psychic emotions with which it had started, and it was also one of the contributory—though not the main—causes of the deterioration of Tantricism.

In their later developments, comprising various sectarian schools, the high idealism of Tantricism and Buddhism was lost sight of, and a gravitation was perceptible in their followers towards vital and, therefore, unspiritual pulls, which betrayed them into the obscurity of dark practices, the perversions of the vital-emotional nature of man. Almost for the same reason Vaishnavism, too, had to remain far from a complete realisation of its great ideal of spiritual humanism, which also figured, but more prominently, as the professed aim of the Tantric and Mahayanist cults evolved in Bengal. Once in her history, however, more notably than on any other occasion, Bengal seemed to have realised that emotion, to be wholly effective, must be steadied and disciplined by knowledge and steeped in the psychic aroma. But the expected result did not come from this attempt that she made by an exclusive exercise of her mind to rationalise the speculations of her peculiar idealism, A system of logic she was no doubt able to build up and a great school of philosophy of all-India fame; but an inordinate emphasis on intellect tended to dry up her heart and wither the natural springs of her emotional being. Happily. however, this was confined to the upper classes and the intellectuals; and when, partly as a reaction to it, the tides of Vaishnavism began to sweep the country from end to end and even beyond its borders, Bengal rediscovered her soul and re-opened her heart. Thus it is emotion again that largely enabled her to respond to the call of Sri Chaitanya and rekindle the sacred flame of Bhakti in her heart.

The variety of her religious adventures should not be understood to mean that Bengal had no fixed ideal to achieve, no one end to pursue. Hindu *sadhana* is based on the idea that though each man has, according to his nature, his own individual line of spiritual development, yet for the supreme perfection of which he is capable he will have to rise to a higher consciousness in which he will see the essential oneness of all the different ways of approaching the Divine, realising at the same time that though each has an end to fulfil, it is all towards the growth of the whole human nature into divine perfection.

That is why a successive pursuit of all these paths or a synthesis of their essentials in an all-englobing Yoga imposes itself upon the seeker of an integral realisation. But as the former is not practicable in the short life and in the defective frame of the individual being, it tended to become a real phenomenon in the long and vigorous life of Bengal's collective being which may be said to have gone successively through all these ways of discipline in different epochs of its history in order, it would seem, to achieve the fullness of its spiritual experience, and thereby grow in its readiness to blossom forth into a more perfect perfection, a freer freedom, and above all, into that sublimer harmony of the future, which is the one solution of the problems that afflict mankind to-day. Thus while a Vedantic zeal for knowledge kindled by the passion of devotion runs through them all like a golden thread, all these paths, each representing an upsurge of human nature, combined to create the Bengal that, in her spiritual life, she is to-day. Vedanta opened her spirit to the Supreme Reality. Through Tantricism, a more practical form of Vedanta, she endeavoured to flower in all the members of her being by receiving into them the Light of the Supreme Shakti. Buddhism, a restatement of the Vedanta in more particular terms of the mind, nourished and provided a wider scope for the fruition of her ethical nature. The culture of the Nyâya logic drilled her intellect into a rationalistic exactitude. In Vaishnavism—whose founder is claimed by the Bengal Vaishnavas as the one real exponent of the Vedanta—and in the cults derived from it, she poured out her whole heart with all the force of her life whose sublimation she attempted in a manner at once striking and singular.

These great successes apart, her failures, too, are not without their meaning: since they are not merely warnings against the repetition of the wrong steps but they also add to the colour and richness of her experiences on which the future will be built.

'Bengal, as we know, did not reject life and its values as illusion. Rather, she tried along the above ways—each in its day a great unifying force—to discover their secret significance, accepting life as a field of spiritual unfolding with the result that an abundance of creative energy was released And impelled by it, she took to those corporate activities that throughout her history have given their unfailing impetus to the growth in her collective life of a unique form of cultural fellowship through which Bengal became one, and realized her oneness with others, with all, with the whole of India, and even with countries outside her, opening thereby into the vision of that harmony, her supreme ideal, that came more clearly to the seeing intuition of her religious consciousness and towards which the soul of Bengal through all its expressions seemed to have been moving from ages past, as if willed by the Dispenser of her destiny.'

BENGAL GREATER THAN HERSELF

It is not true that Bengal in her past was 'nonconformist' or that she chose to live and grow in isolation. The sons of Bengal started from very early times to go out of their country on travels and adventures, on cultural and colonising missions, to various parts of India and even to countries far beyond her geographical boundaries. And it was through these activities that Bengal was able to enlarge the sphere of her cultural fellowship, the story of which has yet to be fully unravelled. Even as we have it now, it is too long for the space that the present occasion can provide. A bare outline of it is, therefore, attempted here giving a few of its more important facts and events as well as a short account of the work of such personalities as have played a more prominent part in building up the cultural fellowship of Bengal in India and abroad.

The rulers of ancient Bengal used to proclaim their paramount authority by assuming the title of *Panchagaudeshuara,* the emperor of the five Gaudas (Bengals) which extended over almost the whole of northern India, showing the vastness of their political influence in the India of old. In their great days the Pala kings of Bengal ruled an empire comprising almost the whole of northern India. A copper-plate inscription, found in Monghyr, says that Devapala, a son of the famous Pala king Dharmapala, annexed the Pandya kingdom of the extreme south and extended his dominion up to Rameswaram. In the Punjab, the ruling families of the small states, Suket, Keonthal, Kashtwar and Mandi, owe their genealogical origin to the 'Rajas of Gauda' in Bengal. The Udichya Brahmins of Gujarat, the Gauda Brahmins of the United Provinces and Central India, the Gauda Brahmins of the South Konkan and Kanada speaking a dialect (Konkani) that in many respects resembles the Bengali language, are descendants of the Bengalis who had migrated to those regions in days long gone by.

In the middle of the ninth century A.D. Avighnakara, an inhabitant of Gauda, went and settled in Krishnagiri (modern Kanheri in the Bombay Presidency) and excavated in the hill there a great monastery for the residence of the monks. Ishanshiva was another Brahmin of Gauda who became the chief of the well-known Shaiva monastery in Vodamayuta (modern Badaun in the United Provinces). A Bengali, named Shaktiswami, became the minister of Lalitaditya of Kashmir during the eighth century. Some of his descendants were reputed men of letters. Lakshmidhara, a well-known poet of Bengal, was a court-poet of the Paramara king Bhoja of Malava in the eleventh century. Halayudha is the name of another Bengali poet who settled in Malava and whose verses are found engraved in the temple of Amareswara in Mandhata in the Nimar district of the Central Provinces. Yet another poet from Bengal who settled in the same country was Madana. He rose to the position of the preceptor of the Paramara king Arjunavarman of the thirteenth century. Abhayakaragupta of Gauda was the head of the Mahayana sect in the Odantapuri monastery which accommodated three thousand monks. He was a reputed writer of books on Tantric Buddhism and translated into Tibetan many authoritative works on the same subject. He is even to-day most highly esteemed in Tibet, being worshipped as one of the Lamas possessing royal dignities.

The origin of the Cheras of south India has been traced to a tribe of Naga-worshippers that migrated from Bengal. The old Tamil literature contains significant references to the close connection that once existed between the peoples of the South, speaking the Dravidian languages, and the people of Bengal. Umapatideva, a great Shaiva teacher of Bengal of the twelfth century, went and settled in the Chola country and there acquired renown for his supernatural powers. It is said that once by worshipping Shiva for twenty-eight days he saved the Chola country from the invasion of a Sinhalese army. Visveswara-shambhu, another Shaiva teacher of Bengal of the thirteenth century, was the chief teacher of the famous Goloki monastery near Jubbulpore in the Central Provinces. He was a famous Vedic scholar.

The Chola and Malava kings were his disciples, as also the Kakatiya king Ganapati of Warangal and a king of the Kalachuri dynasty of Tripuri. He lived for many years in the court of Ganapati who is said to have been his spiritual son. He built a temple, a monastery, a college, a *choultry* for distribution of food, a maternity home and a hospital, in the villages on the banks of the Krishna which he had received as gift from Ganapati. He provided for their maintenance and himself drew up a course of studies for the college covering all branches of Hindu learning. He also built several other temples and monasteries in the Deccan. Chandragomin, the founder of the Chandra school of Sanskrit grammar, was a Kshatriya of Varendra (north Bengal). He went to Ceylon and south India, in both of which he was highly honoured for his great scholarship. Ramachandra Kavibharati, a versatile genius of Bengal, went to Ceylon during the reign of Parakramabahu II in the thirteenth century. There he embraced Buddhism and wrote a number of books for which the king conferred on him the title of Bauddhagamachakravarti. Incidentally, this exodus of Brahmins from Bengal began long ago, but it was occasioned in a later period, once by the rapid rise and popularity of of Buddhism which weakened the Brahmin's influence, and in another instance, by the Muslim invasion of Bengal which gave a rude shaking to the country.

The maritime activity of Bengal had of course its glorious days when in the fourth century B.C. Vijayasinha, an enterprising prince of Bengal, sailed over the rough waters of the Bay and built up a colony in Ceylon whose old name 'Sinhal' is derived from his name. Linguistic and other cultural affinities that still exist between the present Bengalees and the Sinhalese are clear enough in pointing to this ancient bond. Bengal scholars, artists, missionariees. and colonisers crossed the seas in their stately ships and spread the cultural ideals of their motherland in distant countries. The relics and antiquities unearthed in Java, Bali, Cambodia, and Siam bear unmistakable evidence of the stamp on them of the art and culture that these heroic ambassadors of Bengal carried to those far-away regions. An inscription in Java mentions that Kumaraghosha, the preceptor of the Shailendra emperors of Java, was an inhabitant of Gauda. The intimate intercourse between the Pala and the Shailendra kingdoms explains the great influence exercised by the Pala art upon that of Java. Another evidence of the close contact between Java and Bengal is the affinity between the scripts used on certain Javanese sculptures and the proto-Bengali alphabet. This contact continued till at least the fourteenth century A.D. The temple of Boro-Budur, that grand epic of architecture, is the creation of builders from Bengal and Orissa. Many of its designs and sculptures are only adaptations from those of the Paharpur monastery in north Bengal which preceded Boro-Budur by at least a century and a half. Bengalees formed a large percentage of the Bhikshus who, about a thousand, resided in Srivijaya, modern Sumatra, then (early eleventh century) a famous centre of Buddhist learning. Srijnan Dipankar, the renowned Buddhist scholar and saint of Bengal, who was in charge of the University of Vikramshila, visited Srivijaya and was so impressed by it that he declared it as the headquarters of Buddhism in the East. History records in glowing terms the story of how Dipankar, regardless of his poor health, undertook the perilous journey to Tibet at the request of its king and founded there a school of Tantric Buddhism. Even to-day in many monasteries of Tibet Dipankar is worshipped as next to the Buddha. But Dipankar had been preceded by other Bengali scholars among whom the names may be mentioned of Shantarakshita and Padmasambhava who had together visited Tibet in the eighth century and helped in spreading the doctrines of Buddhism there. They both belonged to the University of Nalanda. Shantarakshita was a distinguished philosopher, a logician and an authority on Tantric Buddhism. He also visited Nepal. Padmasambhava was a professor of the Tantras at Nalanda. He is still honoured in Tibet as the founder of Lamaism, the most important religious institution of that country.

Bengal had her share in the propagation not

only of Buddhism, but also of such sectarian cults of Hinduism as Shaivism and Vaishnavism. Many temples and monasteries belonging to these creeds at Prome, Thaton, and Taqang, in Burma, are believed to be the work of Bengali architects. Nor was Bengal unrepresented in the cultural missions that went to China from India. The old paintings in the caves called Tzu-hsia Tung near Nanking and in the famous Pagoda in Kai-fong, in China, depict figures of Indian scholars looking and dressed exactly like Bengali Brahmins, and of religious musical gatherings which resemble in every way the Sankirtana singers of Bengal. The eminent artist, Nandalal Bose who visited these temples, is of opinion that these pictures are without doubt those of Bengalees. Inscriptions, including those of Tantric *mantrams* in Bengali letters in a temple in Peking called Wu Ta-ssu, *i.e.,* roofed over by a group of five spires, which is built almost in the famous Pancharatna (five jewels, *i.e.,* five spires) style of Bengal, are along with the above paintings tangible proofs of Bengal's influence in China. Bengali authorship has been discovered of many of the Sanskrit texts on Tantric Buddhism and Buddhist logic which are now available in Chinese and Tibetan versions in China and Tibet, the originals having been lost in their homeland. Inspiration from Bengal is traced in many of the old sculptures and paintings of Buddhist and Brahminical deities, as well as in certain inscriptions in Bengali characters in the temples at Nara and Horiyuji in Japan. But more interesting is the fact that even to-day the Buddhist priests of the Horiyuji temple write their scriptures not in Sino-Japanese pictorial letters but in those that were prevalent in Bengal during the Pala-Sena period. The art of Bengal exercised a lasting influence on the art of Nepal, Burma, and Ceylon. The style of painting, developed in Bengal, has been discerned in the art of Ajanta, Bagh, and the Kangra valley. The two Bengali masters, Dhiman and Vitpala (ninth century), were the founders of a great school of painting of an all-India fame whose influence travelled to Nepal, China, and Japan. Bengal was also a great creative centre of architecture. The styles of the roofs and gables sculptured at Bharut and Sanchi and painted at Ajanta were originally evolved in Bengal out of the old tradition of bamboo construction peculiar to that country. Many of the constructive forms used at Gauda came to predominate even in the more recent Mogul architecture of Fatehpur-Sikri, Agra, and Delhi. The bent cornices and curvilinear roofs of Gauda, derived from the bamboo construction of old Bengal, are seen in many edifices built by the Moguls and the Rajputs. Influence of Bengal can likewise be traced both in the theme and technique of the Kangra portraits.

The Universities of Nalanda, Vikramshila, and Odantapuri, situated on the frontiers of old

Bengal, were the far-famed centres of learning where the scholars of Bengal came in contact with those from different parts of India. The Pala kings of Bengal extended their high patronage to all of them, as also to the large number of Buddhist monasteries in Bengal where the various schools of Buddhist thought were represented by learned Bhikshus engaged in the joint study and research of their respective philosophies, an intellectual brotherhood of a very high order. Vikramshila developed out of one such monastery, founded by the great Pala king Dharmapala. It was known as a Royal University, its titles being bestowed by kings who presided over its convocations. Its special subject of study was the Tantras and the Tantric cults in which Buddhism in Bengal found its new forms. Vikramshila made a great contribution in the exposition of Tantric thought which helped forward the synthetic fusion of Hinduism and Buddhism. The University of Odantapuri was likewise evolved in another monastery of which Gopala, the first of the Pala kings, was the founder. Ramapala founded the noted centre of learning, called Jagaddalvihar. Vallabhi was another such university in Bengal which has not yet been located.

But the greatest of them all was the international University of Nalanda. It was by far the largest centre of learning in the contemporary world to which scholars of different castes, creeds, and races hailing not only from the farthest ends of India such as Kashmir, Peshawar, Conjeevaram and Samatata but also from countries far beyond, from China, Japan, Korea, Java, Sumatra, Tibet, Mongolia and Bokhara, flocked for carrying on advanced studies in the various branches of knowledge, both Brahminical and Buddhistic. The University had a predominating Bengali element in its population of 10,000, of whom 8,500 were *alumni,* and 1,510 were faculty members. It was famous for the freedom it encouraged in education, for the wide catholicity of its method and for the universal character of its curriculum. Through its discussions, its debates and its conferences, according to the old Indian tradition, Nalanda was surely helping to forge its varied elements into the unity of a superb intellectual fellowship, in which the wide variety of subjects taught was a remarkable feature. The curriculum included all the various systems of thought, Brahminical as well as Buddhistic, in spite of the fact that Nalanda was reputed as a centre of Mahayanist studies. The Vedas, the Upanishads, works of different philosophical systems as Samkhya, Vaisheshika, Nyaya, were studied and taught there as also the arts and sciences of the Hindus. The various schools of Buddhism were represented by their eminent exponents and earnest learners. People belonging to almost all the sects and creeds of the time shared a common cultural life in Nalanda, a cosmopolitan university in the true sense of the term. No wonder that it should have fostered a spirit of creative fellowship among the vast number of its members. The Pala kings were all of them ardent patrons of Nalanda. And the most liberal support and encouragement that it ever received was from Dharmapala in whose time the University reached the height of its glory. But it had, too, a glorious period about a century before when the eminent Bengali scholar Shilabhadra was its distinguished Chancellor. It was with him that the renowned Chinese pilgrim, Hiuen Tsang, came to study the Yoga philosophy at Nalanda. Thus the kings and scholars of Bengal had their full share towards the building up of this University which was only another name for an intellectual brotherhood of a splendid type.

It may be noted that most of these Universities—particularly Nalanda and Vikramshila in the tenth and eleventh centuries—specialised in the study and exposition of the Tantras and helped to transmit their lore to scholars and seekers from various lands. And it is well-known that Bengal developed the philosophy and practice of the Tantras in her own way as the very cult of her soul.

There is ample evidence that Bengal had actively continued in this spirit till early in the thirteenth century, when the Muslim iconoclasts destroyed these abodes of learning. But it cannot be said that the spirit vanished completely from her later educational ventures, though its external manifestation on a large scale was not possible under conditions which were no longer favourable. What actually happened was that the central vastness of the earlier institutions was for obvious reasons replaced by a large number of decentralized *tols* or schools of Sanskrit learning in sequestered villages far away from the urban centres of political turmoil. These schools made distinctly original contributions towards the enrichment of Indian thought, although they were devoted to an exclusive study of the speculative aspects of Brahminical culture. For, Buddhism came within their discussions only when they had had to criticise it for establishing the Brahminical standpoint. It was a period of decline for Buddhist culture which was brought about, first, by the destruction of the universities and monasteries involving the death of a large number of Buddhist scholars, and by the exodus of a large number of them from Bengal; secondly, by the revival of Hindu culture under the patronage of the Sena kings in the twelfth century; and lastly, by the gradual assimilation of Buddhism into the main body of Hinduism. It may, however, be mentioned that the expounders of the neo-Nyâya philosophy of Bengal followed the dialectics of Buddhist logic, though nowhere in their literature so far available any acknowledgment of it is to be found. But the *tols* of Bengal, however humble in comparison with the great centres of Buddhist culture, did, all the same, keep alive the ancient spirit of fellowship through the common corporate life of learning. And of them the most notable was the one founded by Raghunath Shiromoni (sixteenth century?) at Navadwip, for many centuries one of the greatest seats of Sanskrit learning in all India, where scholars from various far-off parts of the country, the Punjab and Kanauj in the north and Tamil-land in the south, used to congregate for studying the Nyâya philosophy of which Raghunath was then the highest acknowledged authority.

Sri Chaitanya's *Digvijaya,* victorious campaigns, in the west as far as Gujarat and in the south as far as Rameswaram, is a glorious chapter in the history of greater Bengal. Fired with a heavenly zeal Chaitanya started out on his holy mission of disseminating the sacred name of God, and conquered by his consummate wisdom and matchless devotion the heart of Vasudeva Sarvabhauma of Puri, one of the foremost scholars of the time, who on hearing Chaitanya's masterly exposition of the Hindu scriptures in the light of his teachings acknowledged him as the Avatâra of the age. Equally successful was his campaign in Gujarat. But more remarkable is what he did in Benares, which was then the most notable centre of Sanskrit learning in the whole of India. An upheaval, as it were, was created in the intellectual world of Benares when its leader Prakashananda Saraswati, the then greatest authority on Vedanta and head of the order of Dandi Sannyâsins, accepted this young Sannyasin from Bengal as his spiritual Guru. The same thing happened in the Deccan where reputed scholars like Chundiram Tirtha felt humbled before the wisdom and devotion of Chaitanya. This God-intoxicated saint used invariably to cover his itinerary on foot. It was indeed a wonderful sight when filled with the ambrosia of pure Bhakti he moved about from place to place in those distant regions of India, meeting their representative thinkers and converting them to his faith, himself singing and ardently praying others to sing the name of Krishna, stretching out his arms of love and brotherhood to one and all, to the poor in the street as well as to the rich in their halls, to hundreds and thousands who, as if attracted by a magnet, flocked to him only to be caught in the intensity of his devotional fervour.

Thus this new cult of Bhakti began to grow in its hold on the religious imagination of people even outside the borders of Bengal. Almost all the chiefs of Orissa adopted it as their faith along with vast masses of people right in the interior of that country. Its most powerful king, Prataparudra, vied with others to be accepted by Chaitanya as one of his humble followers. So did king Rudrapati of Travancore when the Master visited that country. In this way Bengal Vaishnavism came to live, and still lives, in the Vaishnava communities in the Deccan, Gujarat, Orissa, and Brindavan. Within a few years after the passing away of Sri Chaitanya, Navadwip, Puri, and Brindavan became the recognized centres of Vaishnavic discipline and thought, Brindavan being by far the largest of them. Commanded by their Master, some of Chaitanya's disciples who were reputed for their unrivalled scholarship had already gone to Brindavan and established themselves there. Rupa Goswami and Sanatana Goswami figured as the most leading of them who, in collaboration with others including Jiva Goswami, helped to bring back to Brindavan its ancient splendour in which it shines to-day in the religious consciousness of India. Thousands of devotees of all classes from different parts of the country began to gather, as they do now, to receive their initiation in Vaishnavic *Sâdhanâ* and to study its philosophy, both of which were systematized by its distinguished exponents into a literature which is as vast as it is of classical excellence. The temple still stands there. that fine piece of architecture, which was erected by Maharaja Mansingh at the instance of his Gurus, Rupa and Sanatana. The great Mogul emperor Akbar met Rupa and Sanatana, and was so impressed by them that he composed a song in Hindi on Sri Chaitanya. It is not possible to describe in a few words the many ways in which Brindavan has served as a perennial source of inspiration to countless pilgrims and devotees. But the fact is there that it has been during all these centuries a creative centre of fellowship in the domain of religion, built up by the new-found religious enthusiasm of the Bengal Vaishnavas.

What has been said above would, we hope, be enough not only to explode the myth of isolation imputed to Bengal but also to prove that her genius gave marvellous forms to the ideal of fellowship in the realm of religion and culture, both within and without her physical frontiers. And through these undertakings, stupendous as well as incomparable, Bengal became greater than herself, greater even than the ideal which was so dear to her. For to cement bonds of friendship with others through the diffusion of her culture was not her sole purpose: she also wanted to share with them the common effort, for which the synthetic cast of her mind and her emotional heart were so helpful, to arrive at life's fulfilment in the world of sweetness and light, and thereby grow in readiness for a greater life in the future, which indeed is the ultimate aim of her creative strivings.

But Bengal was not only a bestower of her gifts to others. She was plastic enough to take in every healthy influence that came to her from outside. Not everything, however, but everything that is good and beneficial was what she looked for in accepting gifts from others. Her discrimination in this respect was once the cause of her being declared a rebel. The Kshatriya mystics of Bengal did not recognize to a considerable extent the importance of Vedic rituals. And when they expressed their disinclination to honour as Brahmins the priests who merely chanted the Vedic hymns and performed the rituals, there started a feeling of disaffection among the Brahmin priests, many of whom left Bengal and joined their caste-fellows in northern India in running down the Kshatriya ascendancy in Bengal. This priestly obscurantism did not take long to be organized; and when the Kshatriya power began to show a tendency towards decline the former sought to assert its authority by banning any entry of Brahmins into Bengal, proclaiming her as an enemy of the Vedas. Thus Bengal came to be for a long time in the bad books of the so-called Vedic Brahmins who, by an exclusive emphasis on externalism and on the rigidity of caste rules, alienated in a later period vast masses of people in Bengal, contributing thereby to their ready acceptance of the liberal teachings of Jainism and then of Buddhism. The lesson of this, however, is clear. It vindicates the true spirit of Bengal. Bengal wanted the knowledge of Truth, not the paraphernalia of religion. To her a Brahmin was one who had realized in his life the true Truth of the world. Birth was not, to Bengal, a criterion of a man's spiritual worth. That is why in those early days many Kshatriyas in Bengal, as in other parts of India, having attained higher knowledge were elevated to the rank of Brahmins and were honoured by the title of Brahma Kshatrottara, or greater than the Brahmins and the Kshatriyas. It is this ideal for which Bengal has stood through the ages, for which she has striven in all her spiritual endeavours, whether through Vedantic mysticism, the discipline of the Tantras, Buddhism, or of Vaishnavism. It is true that she was not always able to keep to this high standard of spiritual discrimination and that her inability to do so was responsible for many of great failures; but whatever success she did achieve was possible only when she was able among other things to stick to this ideal.

It is well-known that the present Bengalee is the product of the fusion of many ethnic types. But this racial chemistry apart, the cultural intermingling that has taken place in Bengal almost from times prehistoric is apparently an incomparable phenomenon that has worked, more than any other, towards the growth and enrichment of her own culture. It has made her so synthetically minded as to be able to accept truths, whatever their source, and assimilate them into her own being in which they lose their separate identity and become one with the soul and body of the culture that goes by her name. Bengal came in touch with the Indus valley civilization; and there is even an opinion that she had a hand in its creation: the Dravidian culture did leave its impress on her: and it can be safely said that she was influenced by the early Mongolians with whom she came into contact. The Vedic ideals were certainly an exalting element in the creative life of Bengal in which the contribution of Buddhism also was not of little importance. Tantricism, Shaivism, and Vaishnavism were absorbed by her and recreated into the forms in which they are known to-day. The note of Islam also was not excluded from this diapason, neither was that of the culture of the West which Bengal was the first in India to receive. If adequate material evidence is not yet available as to how these different streams of culture were blended into what is creative in the Bengal of to-day, she would certainly live to prove that her success in the past in evolving out of them a culture of her own and her daring efforts to strike out her own individual lines of development, both cultural and spiritual, are not without some meaning for the days to come with a greater glory to illumine the pages of her unborn history. It is as if to fulfil this future possibility that Bengal has stood through the ages, verily as a power of Mother India.

FELLOWSHIP THROUGH AN INTERFUSION OF CULTS

It is not known precisely when Buddhism started to spread in Bengal, but that influence reached its zenith during the four and a half centuries of Pala rule which were remarkable for intellectual and artistic activities of a very high order. The event with which the Palas began shows the democratic tendency in the political consciousness of old Bengal. For Gopala, the founder of the dynasty, became king by the consent and will of the people, a fact which indicates that there was unity in the political life of the time. This is also characterised as an awakening of Bengal to a sense of her nationhood. Buddhism and the great culture that it built up had during the Pala period deeply permeated the mind and heart of Bengal, but the days of its decline began when after the fall of the Palas the Senas (twelfth century) rose as champions of conventional Hinduism, with the result that a reaction set in against the liberating influence of Buddhism on society. The Senas were strict followers of the canons and traditions of their religion, and during their rule the social laws became rigid and proved a hindrance to the collective progress of the people. It must, however, be said to their credit that they endeavoured to re-affirm to the people the greatness and glory of the Hindu ideals, however orthodox might be their way of doing it; and that the solidarity of the people and their loyalty to the rulers made it possible for the latter to enforce those invidious laws including the new caste alignments as formulated by them. There is no denying the fact, that the policy of the Senas was largely responsible for the disintegration that was soon found to be paving the way for the Muslims to invade and conquer Bengal without much resistance. Not only that; as the spirit of the past was not understood in its deeper implications, and as only a mental approach to it was made, and that too by a very small section belonging to the upper ranks in society, the people were left without any large and integral vision to inspire them towards those common, corporate activities that bring real and all-round well-being to a country. Thus the common people, left to themselves, tended to be confined within innumerable folk-forms of culture, and the deterioration of these forms especially in the domain of religion, became glaring in the pre-Chaitanya period.

Nevertheless, the soul of Bengal has scarcely allowed any such adverse condition to continue for a very long time; and it has always struggled, more with success than with failure, to be reborn again and again into new forms of religion and culture. Sri Chaitanya came with his message of neo-Vaishnavism not only to stand against such reactionary forces as were destroying the social and religious life of the people, but also to vindicate the truth of devotion to God as the only truth that can be realized by all, high and low, and for which a heart full of love for the Divine was the only thing necessary. But the Vaishnavism of Bengal was a new orientation of the Bhakti cult, different in tint from the Vaishnavism of the North or of the South, in the same way as the Buddhism that was prevalent in Bengal was not exactly the accepted Buddhism of the rest of India. Dharmapala, a Buddhist by faith and an ardent patron of Buddhist culture, performed Vedic sacrifices and offered liberal gifts to the Brahmins who conducted the sacrifices on his behalf. Many of his ministers were Brahmins.

The stamp that Buddhism left on the religious life of Bengal can be perceived even to-day. It is interesting that many of their deities the Bengali Hindus have received from Buddhism. It is still more interesting to note that these deities had been adapted from Tântricism and Paurânic Hinduism. From both these Mahayana Buddhism, for many centuries the prevailing religion in Bengal, had derived many of its conceptions including those of its anthropomorphic symbolism. Its Yoga and Bhakti cults are distinctly Hindu in their inspiration. Tantric Buddhism which rose to its heights during the Pala period was the source of many cults of Bengal of which an important one is the Sahajiyâ.

Bengal's contribution is unique in the movement that led to the absorption of Buddhism into Hinduism of which the outstanding consequence was the acceptance of the Buddha in Hinduism as one of the ten incarnations of Vishnu. In the religious consciousness of Bengal as in that of other provinces the Buddha yet figures as such. It is under the influence of Tantric Buddhism that the Hindus of Bengal, even now, worship their most popular deities such as Târâ, Kâli and Saraswati. The seven Hindu deities called Ugrâ, Mahogrâ, Vajrâ, etc., are derived from Tara of Buddhism. The Hindus associate the conception of *Akshobhya* (an imperturbable state) and *Ekajatâ* (a single-matted figure) with Tara. But they came immediately from Buddhism. In the Tantra of the Hindus *Akshobhya* is identified with Shiva; whereas in Tantric Buddhism he is the Dhyâni Buddha: *Ekajatâ* also is a Buddhist deity. Saraswati is of course a Vedic deity. But in Bengal she is worshipped as Bhadrakâli who is only a formal variation of the Buddhistic Tara. There are instances of the figure of the Buddha being worshipped by the Hindus in one or other of the many names of Shiva of which Jatâshankar (Shiva with matted hair) is a common one. In a village in Tipperah, an ancient Buddhistic site, a Buddhist icon is worshipped as Krishna.

The Dharma of the Buddhist Trinity still receives offerings from the Hindus in some parts of west Bengal. The Gambhira festival of North

Bengal and the Gajan of West Bengal have their origins in Buddhism. The Dharmaraj Buddha of the Buddhist festivals have now become Shiva. On the other hand, in the Dharma Puja festival, as mentioned in *Sunyapurana,* the Mahayanists used to worship Shiva. There are certain texts in which Buddha and Shiva are together contemplated upon. In Ghanaram's *Dharmamangal* Dharma of Buddhism and Vishnunarayana are regarded as identical. Manik Ganguly addresses Dharma as Govinda-Gopal, Gopinath—names of Krishna—and says that the Vaikuntha is the heavenly residence of Dharma, and Lakshmi is his divine consort. Even now, during the Gajan festival of Bengal, Hindu women go through fast and penances to propitiate Nilavati who is a Buddhist goddess. It is said that Chandidasa's Basulidevi is the Vajreswari of the Buddhists. Adyashakti of the Hindus and the Adya of the Buddhists are the same. Mangalchandi, the popular goddess among the Hindu women, is derived from Adya as described in Manikdutta's *Chandi.* Vajra of the Buddhistic Vajrayana is nothing but the Shakti of the Brahminical Tantra. The twenty-third Digambar Tirthankar of Jainism is in many places worshipped as Shiva. Like Tantricism, Shaivism also played an important part in bringing about a fusion of Hinduism with both Buddhism and Jainism, the latter having preceded the former in being a popular form of religion in some parts of Bengal.

This process of fusion must have begun long ago when Buddhism came in contact with Tantricism, always a dominant cult in Bengal. Most of the deities and doctrines that have given form to Bengal Buddhism, are the product of Tantric reorientation, having very little to do with the original Buddhist cult. The Buddhist goddesses of Bengal are said to be variants of the Tantric conception of Shakti, though, as we have said before, the forms and rituals of their worship to-day are those of Tantric Buddhism to which they once belonged. This goes to show that there was a time when they were common to both Buddhism and Tantricism. Mention may be made here, in passing, that the *Chandi,* one of the most sacred and popular scriptures of the Tantric Hindus, was held in equal esteem by the Tantric Buddhists. A manuscript of it, about a thousand years old and in the handwriting of a Buddhist monk, has been found in Nepal. The *Chandi* is the quintessence of Tantric thought, as the Gita is of Vedantic thought. It consists of thirteen chapters from the *Mârkandeya Purâna* of the Hindus and was written in Bengal during the third century of the present era. Its popularity among both the Hindus and Buddhists indicates that there was an undoubted affinity between these two lines of religious practices and thought. Even the idea of Buddha has taken on a new character in Bengal, and there is a view that the conception of Shiva has played an important part in its elaboration. It is in this inspiration from the Tantras that there is to be found the genesis of the movement through which Buddhism in Bengal began to lose its distinctiveness till it was completely merged into Tantricism or, more correctly, into Tantric school of Hinduism.

This movement was really a gradual process that worked its subtle way into the religious mind of Bengal, manifesting itself in the collaboration towards fusion of the more liberal among the followers of the two cults. A literary evidence of this movement is furnished by *Shunyapurana* (eleventh century?), a treatise on the Dharma cult which is a degenerate form of the Mahayana creed and to which we have already referred as being still prevalent in some parts of Bengal in a Hindu garb. The cosmogonical theories, stated in that work, are only an echo of what the *Rigveda* and the Tantras say on the same subject, and there have also crept into them such Brahminical gods as Brahmâ and Vishnu along with various Pauranic ideas.

It is not difficult to imagine how in this way a wonderful religious fellowship was developing among the Tantric and Buddhist communities in Bengal in those early days. During the Sena period the people were so much steeped in Buddhistic and Tantric ideas that in order to bring them back to the Hindu fold the revivalists of orthodox Hinduism were forced to re-interpret the conception of Shiva as having all the attributes with which the Buddha was idealized, as also to introduce those rituals and modes of worship which were common to Tantricism and Buddhism. Such compromises have, by no means, been rare in the history of religions. Vedic leanings, we have seen, were connived at by the early Buddhists of Bengal. The non-Aryan element in the Aryan pantheon is associated with the efforts that were made in early times to absorb the non-Aryans into the Aryan fold. Mithraism (the cult of Sun-worship) was so deep-rooted in the religious consciousness of pre-Christian Europe that the early fathers of Christianity found it impossible to dissuade the new converts from observing Mithra rites and had, therefore, to shift back the celebration of Christmas from its previous date, the sixth of January, to the twenty-fifth of December, the winter solstice (according to Julian Calendar), which date was the commencement of the annual festival of Mithraism, in which the early Christians would invariably participate. Thus the Nativity of the Sun came to be identified with the Nativity of the Christ.

It is difficult, if not impossible, to have a complete knowledge of Bengal's past without an understanding of the part played by Tantricism in its making. Ethnologically, Tantric cults were an important factor in the process of Bengal's Aryanization. Culturally, the Tantric idea of the world being a manifestation of the All-blissful

Mother, and, the life of man a ready field for that divine efflorescence, has always been an inspiration for Bengal to break into those creative adventures whose fruits are the constituent elements of her culture. Spiritually, through the practice of Tantric discipline Bengal tried to open up in herself the magazine of divine power and effect by it the conquest and conversion of the lower nature. It is true that Bengal was not able to achieve in her community life the supreme ideal of her Tantric *Sâdhanâ,* and that, because of the attempt in it being made sometimes without proper guidance to bring down power from above into unready and imperfect vehicles and for the satisfaction of the demands of the lower nature—so luring and so difficult to avoid in Tantric practices—it could not always keep to a strict observance of its principles, and in some cases, degenerated into forms that have brought ignominy not only on the few, but unjustly on the whole of this great spiritual discipline. Nevertheless, a little insight will make us realise that Bengal's inner growth in the past and her vision of spiritual possibility in the future, were almost entirely due to her Tantric *Sâdhanâ* to the worship of the Divine Mother, kept alive in the life of the race by generation after generation of pure selfless seekers who by their intense *Sâdhanâ* preserved the knowledge. But what is of more importance to our subject is the other fact that by emphasizing the collective aspect of the *Sâdhanâ* in which different natures striving towards a common goal find their unity in an utter surrender to Mahâmâyâ—the basic principle of the Tantra—it laid the foundation of a new spiritual brotherhood—peculiar to Bengal—which gave a social meaning to her Tantric culture.

In a sense the Tantra is a synthesis of Hinduism. If Vedanta is its beginning, the Tantra is its end. For it does not stop with the realization of the Infinite ; it also seeks to arrive at the realization on earth of an infinite existence, a Divine birth—which is the esoteric significance of the Vedic teaching. The *Bhâgavata* recognizes the necessity of Tantric initiation for all the five principal classes of worshippers. The root Mantras are all Tantric. And in the system of Tantric discipline a wonderful co-ordination is seen of Karma, Yoga, Jnâna, and Bhakti. Almost all the religious and cultural movements in Bengal from early times to the present day have behind them some kind of Tantric inspiration. While its practice throughout the ages has given Bengal her synthetic mind, her catholic outlook, her vision of harmony, its influence is not difficult to perceive in the efforts that she has made towards her spiritual and cultural advancement. Vedanta provided her with the grounding on which Tantricism itself developed. The Buddhism of Bengal, as we have seen, was essentially a Tantric cult. Her ancient seats of learning were many of them at least famous for their Tantric studies.

Bengal's cultural fellowship with foreign countries including Nepal, China and Japan was cemented through the propagation mostly of her Tantric doctrines. Even in the texture of the neo Vaishnavic thought Tantric elements are traceable.

During the time of Sri Chaitanya a large number of sects and schools many of which derived from Tantric Buddhism, existed in the country. Some of them were absorbed by the new movement and a few continued as before. But there were also those who in their quiet conclaves kept burning the fire of Tantric *Sādhanā*, its root-word and its thought. When the modern age dawned in India the impact of Western culture which Bengal was the first to receive, brought about conditions which compelled her to look back to the past and restore some of the imperishable treasures of her ancient culture and thereby get ready for the renaissance of her spirit that had been heralded by the efforts of her inspired sons. The rediscovery of the spirit of her distinctive culture came to Bengal soon enough and she rekindled in herself an ardent aspiration for the perfection, envisaged in the Agamas. We see this aspiration seeking to define itself inchoately, in those early movements which furthered in a remarkable manner the cause of cultural fellowship towards the building up of a new synthetic culture.

CULTURAL FELLOWSHIP IN MEDIEVAL BENGAL

That the invasion of India by the Afghans was a disturbing factor in the political life of the country will be admitted on all hands. But the view is not always true that the culture and religion of Islam gave a similar shock to the people of India. As a matter of fact Islamic thought had entered India long before any Muslims became rulers in this country. Islam had already begun to be preached and propagated by its saints and mystics, and not by such of its champions who at a later period established political sway over India and used it for imposing their faith on a conquered people. So far, the earliest date of the existence in India of these Muslim saints is ascribed to the eleventh century, though evidence is not wanting that the country had been visited by them even during the previous century and a half. Most of these devotees of Islam were Sufi mystics who, by their austere life and liberal teachings, became very popular among the Hindus many of whom, especially those who were deprived of ordinary human rights by iniquitous social laws, accepted Islam or became ardent admirers of that faith.

In the core of its teachings Islam says nothing which Hinduism cannot accept. Besides, the respectful utterance of the Prophet, "I smell a sweet breeze of Allah's knowledge blowing from India," can only imply that the spiritual treasures of India were not unknown to him. It is quite possible that the Muslim saints, at least some of them, came to India not only as preachers of their faith but also as seekers of truth, inspired by the saying of their great Prophet. The doctrines of Sufism were in many respects similar to those of Hindu religious thought. Its emphasis on love for the Divine is believed by some to be an echo of the Bhakti cult of Hinduism. There is even an opinion that Hindu and to some extent Buddhist influence is traceable in the texture of Sufi idealism. These facts were not a little responsible for the success that attended the efforts of the early Muslim preachers in India. In Bengal, naturally inclined to Bhakti, these Fakirs found their task easy enough. They were themselves men of faith, and their teachings accentuated by the fervency of their devotion touched the heart of Bengal and ensured for them a warm welcome. Hundreds of her children keenly followed the Sufi's message which they took to be a message for all, irrespective of caste, creed or race, with the result that many of them, of whom a fair number consisted of those who were not quite within the pale of the rigid Hindu society, adopted the new faith; and there began that movement of cultural fellowship which Bengal kept up in her characteristic way so that her own culture might be enriched, her own progress accelerated. It would not be wholly correct to say that this movement had always a smooth passage. It had to encounter conflicts, face odds and tackle unfavourable conditions. But a deeper view reveals that behind everything, and inspite of what might seem outwardly to be hostile conditions, both the communities were growing into a tendency to realise their essential oneness in the realm of culture. In what follows are given some facts and events that point to that inherent inclination of the collective soul of Bengal.

I

Ibn Batuta speaks of as many as one hundred and fifty seats of Muslim Fakirs in Bengal about the middle of the fourteenth century when the liberal-minded Fakhruddin was ruling that kingdom. It is not known when exactly these Muslim saints had begun to come into Bengal; but from the number of their seats and the wide influence they exercised on the people when Ibn Batuta visited the country it seems quite possible that they had been there for quite a long time before. For, they had by then been able to extend the sphere of their activity over almost the whole of Bengal, from Pandua in the district of Hooghly in the south-west to Sylhet in Assam in the north-east. We have evidence of existence of quite a number of these saints in Bengal towards the close of the thirteenth century. Only two of them we shall mention here, each of whom chose as his seat either of the extremities of the above sphere of Islamic influence in Bengal. In the then prosperous region of Pandua lived and preached Shah Sufi Sultan whose popularity among the Hindus is borne out by the fact that even to-day Brahmin priests go and show their respects to his tomb in Pandua by ringing bells and gongs used in Hindu religious worship. And this they do just when the call for evening prayer is sent forth from the adjoining mosque which is as old as the tomb of the saint. The other Muslim Fakir was Shah-Jalal who was an Arab belonging to the province of Yemen. It is said that his spiritual guide, when Shah-Jalal was taking leave of him, gave him a handful of dust saying that he should know that place to be the centre of his work whose dust would be similar to the handful that he had given him, in colour, taste and smell. In the course of his itinerary Shah-Jalal came to Sylhet and settled there, as he found the dust of the place having the requisite qualities. This saint possessed miraculous powers and had numerous Hindu admirers; it is said that a Hindu king tested these powers and, convinced of their genuineness, accepted his discipleship along with his son. Incidentally it may be mentioned here that in those early days and even in much later times many Hindus used freely to take spiritual help from these Fakirs; and instances were not rare of their being the accepted Gurus of many Hindus. Shah-Jalal met the famous Sufi Nizamuddin Aulia of Delhi who presented him with a pair of grey pigeons. When he returned to Sylhet with those pigeons, he reared them up with great care as they were the token of his spiritual friendship with the great saint of Delhi. These pigeons grew in number and spread over all parts of East Bengal. The popularity of Shah-Jalal and the esteem in which he is still held in eastern Bengal are testified to by the fact that even to-day grey pigeons are particularly taken care of by every householder, Muslim or Hindu, who considers it a sin to do any injury to them, believing at the same time that he in whose house these *Jalali* pigeons would build their nests would become the favourite of the goddess of fortune, and he whose house they would leave would be forsaken by the same goddess.

In the early days of Afghan rule in Bengal, there were Muslims, some of whom were actual rulers, who venerated Hindu saints. Shamsuddin who ruled Bengal about the middle of the fourteenth century was then at war with the Delhi Sultanate, and his fort at Ekdalia was invested by Firoz Tughluq. While confined in that fort, Shamsuddin was informed of the death of his Hindu preceptor named Bhavani who lived near by. The king was so moved by this news that, regardless of the danger and risk, he went out of the fort in the guise of a Fakir and proceeded straight to the Asram of Bhavani, paid his last homage to the dead body of his preceptor and returned to the fort without being detected. When Firoz came to know of this, he was incensed with rage but at the same time expressed his admiration for Shamsuddin's amazing courage and exemplary devotion to his spiritual master.

In the ballads of East Bengal, many of which were composed by Muslim poets, there are abundant references to the feelings of amity that for centuries had been helping to coalesce Hindus and Muslims into a common social and cultural confraternity. Many of these Muslim poets used to begin their compositions by invoking the blessings of the Hindu gods and goddesses as well as of Allah, and when paying respects to Mecca they would scarcely forget the Hindu sacred place. Kashi. A Muslim poet of Chittagong commenced a ballad by praying for the blessings of all the local Hindu deities and concluded by admiring the greatness of Sita of the Hindu epic, the Ramayana. Another Muslim poet mentioned Jagannath of Puri immediately after Mecca. During the reign of Husain Shah (early sixteenth century) Hindu-Muslim relations took a definite turn towards a new synthesis both in the cultural and religious life of the country. Husain Shah was a great patron of the art and literature of Bengal. And his name is still cherished in Bengal for the efforts that he made to bring together

Hindus and Muslims through a common religious sentiment. He was in that respect the fore-runner of Akbar and his success may be claimed to have been no less, if not greater than Akbar's. Even to this day both Hindus and Muslims worship the common deity called *Satya-Pir,* a cult with which Husain Shah's name is associated as originator. *Satya* is a Sanskrit word for truth and *Pir* is an Arabic equivalent for the Hindu conception of Guru, the Master. The cult of *Satya-Pir* has long been one of the most popular forms of religious worship amongst Hindus and Muslims in Bengal, and the consecrated food at this religious ceremony is called not by the Hindu name of *prasâd* but by the Muslim name of *sinni* which is derived from the Persian word *sireen,* meaning sweet. The religious literature of Bengal has preserved several poems by Hindu and Muslim poets recounting the life of *Satya-Pir* and which are read as part of the ceremonials in connection with his worship, a fact which shows the hold the cult had and still has on the imagination of the people of both the communities.

But *Satya-Pir* is not the only cult evolved in the synthetic soil of Bengal. There are several other folk-forms of worship that have been in vogue in Bengal both among the Hindus and Muslims for a long time past. *Manik-Pir* and *Kalu-Ghazi* are worshipped by both the communities. *Olai-Chandi* is one such goddess of terror who is propitiated by the Hindu and

Muslim masses in order to avoid being victims of her wrath which is believed to be the cause of cruel epidemics. *Tinlakh-Pir* is none else than the Trailakshanath (Trinath?) of the Hindus. The followers of the *Neḍa-Pir* of North Bengal identify Muhammad with Mahadeva, and Fatima with Mahamaya. The influence of Hindu folk-literature on the Muslims of Bengal is unmistakable. Hindu stories used to be told in Muslim houses along with Islamic tales. Sometimes this mixing up of stories from the two sources resulted in the formation of a new type, such as the story of the struggle between a certain Ghazi and Hanuman. Moreover, ballads written in praise of Hindu chiefs, like Raja Sitaram Roy of Bhushna, were recited with enthusiasm in Muslim houses. It is needless to multiply instances of this kind of fellowship in the domain of religion which is a remarkable phase in the Hndu-Muslim relations in Bengal. An inherent tendency, towards synthesis and harmony had always been there; and it took a new turn when Bengal came into contact with Islam. This resulted in the growth of almost a common religious consciousness in the two communities, so much so, that, in time, "many a Mahomedan offered *puja* at Hindu temples, as the Hindus offered *sinni* at Mahomedan mosques". Mirza Hosen Ali, a native of the Tipperah district, who lived a hundred years ago, not only composed songs in praise of the Hindu goddess Kali, but worshipped her at his house with great pomp; and Gariv Hosen Chaudhuri, a contemporary of the Mirza, another Mahomedan Zemindar, was a devout worshipper of Sitala Devi, the goddess of small-pox, worshipped by the Hindus. . . . Hindus have borne Mahomedan names, and the Mahomedans are often called by Hindu names; and such instances are very common even now." Magan Thakur was a distinctly Hindu name of the Muslim Chief Minister of the King of Arakan. Badruddin Pandit, the famous Muslim ministrel of north Bengal, was honoured by the Hindus with the title of Pandit for his wonderful capacity of singing ballads on the heroes and heroines of the Ramayana. Participation by Muslims in the Durga Puja festival of the Hindus, and that by Hindus (in many cases Brahmins) as wrestlers and lathi-players in the Muhurram, was a common phenomenon everywhere in Bengal only a couple of decades ago. A curious custom is seen even to-day that for minor ailments of their children and even of their own, Hindu women stand at the doors of the mosques and hold up little water-pots that devout Muslims may utter Koranic benedictions as they come out after their prayers. A reference may not be out of place here to the munificence, for religious purposes, of the Bengalis, both Muslims and Hindus, in the past, which was prompted entirely by feelings of fraternity and fellowship. The number was not small of Muslim landlords erecting temples for

Hindu deities and making liberal grants for their maintenance as well as for the celebration of necessary festivities, and of Hindu landlords spending money lavishly on the construction of mosques and tombs of the Muslims. Husain Shah restored many Hindu temples of Navadwip. The Shahshuja Mosque in the town of Comilla built by the Hindu Maharaja Govinda Manikya (1658 A. D.) of Tripura, and the temple of Kali in Narayanpur, erected by Mirza Hosen Ali, already referred to, are, by no means, solitary instances.

No less remarkable, rather more peculiar, was the contact that tended to develop between the two communities through inter-communal marriages. Whatever the reason, most Pathans were keen on marrying the daughters of the country which they had adopted. The romantic story of Shamsuddin's *nika* (widow marriage in Islam) with the Hindu widow Fulmati is a well-known instance. Fulmati was a woman of exceptional intelligence and exercised great influence in administrative affairs. It is said that through her help many Hindus held responsible offices in the court. The marriage of the two sons of the highly respectable Brahmin Raja of Ektakia with the daughters of Sultan Husain Shah is an interesting episode in the Hindu-Muslim inter-mingling of blood. On one occasion the Brahmin Raja came to see the Sultan accompanied by his two young sons who were as bright as they were educated. Husain Shah took a fancy to them and expressed his desire to their father to marry his two daughters to them, offering that, as he did not like the Hindu princes to change their faith, his daughters would change theirs and become Hindus, in case they were accepted by the Hindu Raja. Ultimately, however, the Hindu princes changed their religion and married the Sultan's daughters. But the episode did not end here. The Sultan went so far as to marry as many as eleven members of his family including his sons and nephews to the daughters of that Hindu king's family. Muslim folk-songs celebrate another romance. Bhagirath, the Kshatriya Chief of a small territory in Ayodhya, once came to Bengal on pilgrimage and contracted friendship with Ghiasuddin, the then Sultan of Bengal. His intimacy with the Sultan so deepened that he accepted the Sultan's dewanship and settled in Bengal. Later on, one of his descendants, Kalidas by name, a handsome young man, so captivated a daughter of the then Sultan that she desired to marry him. The marriage was hastened after Kalidas had been forced to accept Islam. Another version is that Kalidas, convinced by Muslim scholars of the greatness of Islam, adopted that faith of his own accord. But more interest attaches to this marriage in that its issue was the famous Isha Khan, one of those twelve powerful chiefs of Bengal who displayed exemplary courage in vindicating the independence of their motherland against the aggressive efforts of the Mughal

Emperors of Delhi. Even to-day the descendants of Isha Khan introduce themselves as members of the Dewan family of Jangalbari, tracing their genealogy to Bhagirath.

The contribution of Muslim rulers and under their patronage, that of Hindus and Muslims generally towards the development of Bengali literature has been acknowledged as immense and inestimable. An authority on the history of Bengali literature goes so far as to express his doubt if Bengali literature could have made such progress as it claims to its credit to-day had not the Muslims taken up its cause and given the best of their intellect and energy towards its growth and development. The Sena kings of Bengal were patrons of Sanskrit learning; but the general tendency among the masses, most of whom were either yet Buddhists or not completely Hinduised, was to find some easier medium through which they might be able to acquaint themselves with the ancient lore. The Afghan rulers of Bengal helped in meeting this demand by extending their active patronage to Hindu writers and poets and by commissioning them with the work of translating into Bengali the Hindu epics and the Purânas. Nasir Shah who ruled Bengal for forty years till 1325 was the first to take up the translation of the Mahâbhârata into Bengali. Husain Shah appointed Maladhar Basu, the reputed Hindu poet of the time, to translate the Sanskrit *Bhâgavata* into Bengali in

1480. Maladhar was honoured by him with the title of Gunaraja Khan. Husain Shah used to listen to the reading of the Bengali Mahâbhârata every day. The writings of the celebrated poets, Vijay Gupta and Yasoraj Khan, also patronised by Husain Khan, are full of panegyrics for the Sultan. Like his master, Parâgal Khan, a governor under Husain Shah, was also a patron of Bengali literature. He appointed Kavindra Parameswara, another poet of the time, to translate the Mahâbhârata. Parâgal Khan's son Chhuti Khan, governor of Chittagong, had the *Ashwamedha Parva* of the Mahâbhârata translated into Bengali by the poet Srikaran Naddi. These are only a few instances out of a large number which shows the Muslim rulers' patronage of Bengali literature.

It might also be interesting to note that in the old Bengali compositions of the Muslims there are abundant references to Hindu gods and goddesses. The Hindus also in their writings were, by no means, untouched by Islamic ideas. These writings contain positive indications that a common religious sentiment was growing among both the communities. Thus, Shamsher Ghazi, the Muslim hero of the ballads called *Shamsher Ghazir Gân*, is described as having had, on the eve of a campaign against the state of Tipperah, a dream in which he saw the image of the goddess Kali, worshipped in that state, asking for offerings from the Ghazi if he wanted success in the campaign. The Ghazi did not respond at once. But when the dream was repeated for the third time, the Ghazi had the desired offerings made to that Hindu goddess on his behalf by a competent Brahmin; and his ambition was fulfilled in that he became the master of Tipperah. In a work called *Iman Yatrar Punthi,* the Muslim author addresses a hymn to Saraswati, the Hindu goddess of learning. Karimullah in his *Yamini Vahal* describes a Muslim praying to the Hindu god Shiva. Aftabuddin, the poet of *Jamil Dilram,* sends his hero to the nether world to seek a boon from the *Saptarsis,* the seven sages of the Hindu mythology. Hamidullah in his *Behula Sundari* describes Brahmins consulting the Koran to find an auspicious day. And the Hindu poet Kshemananda in his *Manasâr Bhâsân* mentions the Koran as one of the sacred things that were kept with himself by Lakhindar, a Hindu prince, as protection against a calamity that threatened him. It is no longer disputed that Bharatchandra's *Vidyasundar* was written under Persian influence. The whole story, according to some scholars, is an adaptation in Bengali of a Persian love-story. The old Bengali literature, one of the main sources of this section of our study, is replete with instances of Hindu-Muslim fellowship in the domain of culture. Mention may be made here in passing that many of the early Muslims in Bengal were interested in Sanskrit learning. Daraf Khan's *Ganga-Stotra,* a hymn to Mother

Ganges in Sanskrit, is still chanted by many pious Hindus in various parts of Bengal. The *Padmâvat*, a Bengali translation by Alowal (sixteenth century) of Mir Muhammad Jaisi's Hindi original describing the Alauddin-Padmini episode, shows the Muslim poet's mastery of Sanskrit in that he closely follows the original poem in his use of Sanskrit and Prakrita compound words. The poem gives a very intimate insight into the social life of the Hindus of the time, and inspite of its Sanskritic Bengali, is even to-day recited before large Muslim gatherings in the district of Chittagong./

II

Sri Chaitanya stirred Bengal into a new life of religious enthusiasm which swept away the barriers of iniquitous social laws, so much so that even Muslims were admitted into the fold of Neo-Vaishnavism founded by him. The call of this inspired God-lover was irresistible. Thousands of men and women responded to it, thousands felt thrilled in their hearts as they witnessed the great master falling into an ecstatic trance, chanting the holy name of Krishna. There was no distinction of caste, creed or race in this new cult of spiritual fellowship, broad-based on love,—love that conquared everything and united diverse elements into a singleness of purpose which to Sri Chaitanya was the impassioned adoration of the Personal Divine. Thus the high and the low, the saint and the sinner, every one was welcome to sing the name of God, every one who had humility and devotion was welcome to accept the Lord as the be-all and end-all of his life. This flaming love of God developed into a fervent religious impulse of an amazing intensity whose contagion was difficult to avoid wherever even a spark of it was caught by the naturally emotional heart of Bengal. A large section of the population was still Buddhistic in its inclinations. Hundreds of these as well as many who were not yet within the fold of orthodox Hinduism became Vaishnavas. The Order of Buddhism in Bengal had been split up into several sects and communities, many adopting Tantric discipline and others some easier forms of religious practice, a number of which had deteriorated to libertinism in the name of spiritual liberty. The religious life of the country was in a state of disintegration. The intellectuals were engaged in arid and fruitless disquisitions on the dry problems of logic, and the vast masses of people were wavering between one creed and another, divided by a number of folk-forms of religion which were, many of them, either debased or given to an exclusive externalism having lost all living touch with their spiritual sources. Sri Chaitanya came and instilled into these spiritually helpless people a new fervour and a new hope. But his greatest achievement, which was the crying need of the time. was the unification of men holding different and conflicting beliefs into one religious community. High-caste Brahmins and men condemned to a very low status in society and even those who had no caste at all and those who were outside the Hindu fold,—all were regarded as equals in the new order of the Vaishnavism. Thus was it possible to incorporate into this new community several despised sects which were wallowing in low forms of degenerate Buddhism. A very notable instance of it is furnished by the fact that Virabhadra, son of Nityananda the great companion of Chaitanya, reclaimed at a time as many as two thousand five hundred persons of both sexes by bringing them under the banner of Vaishnavism.

The cult of Sahajiya was widely popular in Bengal. Many people belonging to it, but with a leaning towards Vaishnavic practices, were known as Vaishnavas. Sahajiya recognised no caste or racial distinctions. A section of its followers had a Muslim named Saheb Dhani as its leading preceptor. It is still called by his name, and consists of Hindus and Muslims who go so far as to eat from the same plate. Even to-day it has several centres in the district of Nadia. It does not worship idols, and the members of it are so devoted to one another that one would go to the length of sacrificing one's life for the sake of a brother-in-faith. Sahajiya Vaishnavism attempted a peculiar religious universalism, if such a term can be used. It had in its fold Hindus, Muslims. and even Christians. Pagal Nathi and Gobra sects also recognise no difference between races and castes and have, besides Hindus of all castes. hundreds of Muslims as their followers; and occasions certainly were not rare when they were led and guided by Muslims or Hindus of low birth. So also were the other schools like Khusi Viswasi, Ramballabhi, Jagamohini, Balarami. Neḍa or the shaven, Aul-Baul-Darbes-Sain. Samyogi; in each of these, Hindus and Muslims were considered one as members of a common spiritual fellowship. They did not believe in castes or sects, temples or images, and were, to a certain extent, influenced by Islam, though originally they were variations of the esoteric aspects of Buddhism, Tantricism, or the Vaishnavic forms of Hinduism. But the most influential of the Sahajiya schools was the one founded by Baba Aul. It was likewise made up of Hindus, Muslims and Christians, and was guided by high moral ideals; many of its leaders were men of exemplary character. One who has no complete mastery over one's sex cannot be a true *Kartâbhajâ*, by which name its members came to be known. It created a peculiar language to express its mystic discipline which, in the main, was the exaltation of the natural impulses of man, of which love is the crown, by absolute desirelessness and perfect self-control; so much so that a kind of spiritual and pure intimacy was permitted between man and woman with the idea that such intimacy might help forward their progress towards freedom and perfection, the end of their spiritual seeking. It was assumed that these Sâdhakas, men as well as women, had transcended sexual passions. But human nature as such could not attain to the consummation aimed at merely by a sublimation and exaltation of the vital-emotional nature. Only a complete change, a radical and integral conversion of nature, could lift up the consciousness of man beyond itself. But that was not, neither was any attempt made in that direction; and the result was that it sank into obscure and corrupt practices. Nevertheless, it must be admitted that Sahajiya Sâdhanâ was a very daring and bold experiment and that its early followers were men of high spiritual worth. And no less remarkable was the marvellous spirit of fellowship it fostered among its adherents hailing from so many different castes and creeds.

Adverting to Husain Shah and Chaitanya, we find a wonderful attitude of reverence on the part of the Sultan of Gauda towards the great Vaishnava saint. But it did not come all of a sudden. The *Chaitanya Charitamrita,* a work on the life and teachings of Sri Chaitanya written within a century of his passing away, describes in detail how Husain Shah had been watching the activities of Chaitanya and his rapidly growing influence among all classes of people, how his eagerness was increasing to know more about this great teacher of divine love, and how, at last, the Sultan felt so powerfully attracted to Chaitanya that he exclaimed one day, "To my mind this Chaitanya is God himself personified." The Muslim Qazi and the *sankirtan*-procession episode is another instance of Muslim appreciation of Sri Chaitanya's saintliness. The Brahmin orthodoxy of Navadwip was against the liberal teachings of Chaitanya and decried his *sankirtan*-processions as noisy demonstrations. They represented their grievances to the Qazi who issued an order forbidding these processions. Chaitanya, defying the order, started the procession at the very door of the Qazi. The Qazi came out in rage to demand an explanation, but the sight of young Nimai (Chaitanya's family name) standing in the midst of a crowd with his face lit up with divine ecstasy so moved him that he forthwith embraced Nimai and exchanged but sweet words with him.

Sri Chaitanya admitted into his order several Pathans who were convinced of the truth of his message with the help of arguments based on Muslim scriptures. They are called Pathan Vaishnavas in the *Chaitanya Charitâmrita*. The renowned, Pathan General and Arabic scholar Bijuli Khan was a devout follower of Chaitanya. The esteem with which Haridas, a Muslim, but one of the inner circle of Chaitanya, was held during his lifetime and is still held by the Vaishnavas, is a glowing testimony to the fact that true spirituality is above all separatist barriers created by caste, creed or race. Chaitanya and his companions fully recognised the spiritual greatness of Haridas, and they had no hesitation,—as also, it is said, many Vaishnava Brahmins of the time,—to dine with him on festive occasions. Even at such orthodox rites as a *srâdh* ceremony in a Brahmin home, this Muslim saint used to be the recipient of the same gifts and honours as were offered to respectable Brahmins. When Haridas was on his deathbed, all his companions, Brahmins as well as others, partook at the desire of Chaitanya himself according to the usual Hindu custom, of the sacred water with which Haridas's feet had been washed.

It would not be inopportune to mention that Vaishnavic thought and the doctrines in which it expressed itself were an essential factor in the development of a catholic religious consciousness in many Muslim poets and thinkers. Among the writers of Vaishnavic poetry at least eleven were Muslims. One of them, Garib Khan, is not merely credited with the authorship of a large number of typically Vaishnavic poems, but had also, as his writings show, an intimate acquaintance with the spiritual discipline of the Vaishnavas and the esoteric significance of Chaitanya's advent as the incarnation of Krishna-consciousness as conceived by Radha. Shah Akbar and Aliraj *alias* Kanu Fakir were two Vaishnavic poets and both of them were imbued with the idea of a fundamental unity between Vaishnavism and Islam. In his book called *Jnansàgar* the devout Aliraj describes the oneness of all divine manifestation and speaks of Muhammad and Chaitanya as the inspired devotees of the same God who revealed himself through them for the accomplishment of some purpose in the cosmic play. Not only this, many Islamic ideas on God and god-men are mentioned by another Muslim poet, Saiyad Muhammad Akbar (1657 A.D.). along with what to him were their Hindu equivalents. in the invocation of a long poem which, together with his other works. have been discussed by Dr. Enamul Huq and Maulavi Abdul Karim in their book in Bengali on Bengali literature in the Court of Arakan. The Muslim poet points out in that invocation the ideological similarities between Islam and Hinduism, saying that the Ferista (the Angel) of the Koran is Narada of the Hindu Puranas; Allah is the Ishwara; Payagambar is the Avatar; Adam is Shiva: Eve is Kali; Muhammad is Chaitanya; Khaja Khijir is Vasudeva; the companions of the Prophet are the early playmates of Krishna; Muslim saints are the Munis (sages); the Koran is the Purana; Pir is Guru. A more positive proof is not necessary of the breadth of vision of these Muslim poets and of the largeness of their religious outlook—unavoidably tinctured here and there with certain imaginative vagaries—which enabled them to look beyond the apparent diversities of this world and realise their unity in the ultimate Truth.

Evidences of Islamic influence on the Hindus of Bengal during early Muslim rule are not rare. We have already made references to it. A notable instance indicating how deep it was even on the intellectual aristocracy of the time is found in the pre-Vaishnavic career of Rupa and Sanatan, the well-known companions of Chaitanya, belonging to his inner circle. Rupa and Sanatan were brothers, descendants of a royal Brahmin family of the Deccan. Compelled by untoward circumstances, they came to Bengal and accepted service under Husain Shah who was their father's friend. Sanatan became the Sultan's Chief Minister and Rupa took charge of the literary department of the Court. They were both well-versed in Sanskrit, Arabic and Persian. Rupa had an extraordinary poetical talent and composed several dramas in Sanskrit, while Sanatan's learning ranked him as one of the very few savants of the time. But they had also an intimate knowledge of the teachings of the Prophet and their Islamic inclinations were such that they took Muslim names and preferred to be called by them, Rupa as Dabir Khas, and Sanatan as Sâkar Mallik. The Muslims also were not uninfluenced by the Hindu ways of life. In the book on Bengali literature in the Court of Arakan, already referred to, the authors have shown with the help of books and manuscripts written by Muslims that during the seventeenth century many Hindu customs, especially those followed in the marriage ceremonies, were in vogue among the Muslims of East Bengal. Muslim women used to have on their forehead the vermilion mark like the Hindus; and the Hindu way of showing respects to superiors, the use of Hindu auspicious symbols were not unusual among the Muslims.

During the Mughal rule the religious impulse which Vaishnavism and Islam had combined to inspire in the emotional heart of Bengal became more settled, but its expression in the external life of the people was less prominent owing as some believe, to the apparent indifference and lack of proper patronage and sympathy on the part of the powers that be. Nevertheless, the two communities lived in amity and had scarcely any occasion to be alienated from each other except on purely personal or selfish grounds, as in the case of several wealthy Hindus who betrayed Sirajuddowla by joining with his Muslim enemies and thereby helped in precipitating his ruin which brought irretrievable disaster to the whole country. On the other hand, *Mutakharain* contains many references to Hindus offering willing co-operation to the Muslim rulers both in times of peace and war. Yasawanta Rao of Dacca was a trusted friend and adviser of Nawab Sarafraj Khan. Nawab Alivardi's Chief Minister was the Hindu Durlabhram who revolted against Sirajuddowla when the latter began to ignore him and preferred in important matters of the state the advice of Mohanlal, a Hindu young man well-versed in the arts of peace and war. History will never forget the exemplary courage with which Mohanlal fought for Siraj, for his country, in the battle of Plassey. When the Mahratta raids in Bengal became extremely distressing for Alivardi a Hindu friend of the Nawab came and offered to take him to a place of safety. Alivardi followed him, but the way that they took was a wrong one, and when the Hindu friend came to know of it, he was so repentant that he killed himself with his own sword. *Muzaffarnama* relates that in the time of Alivardi many members of his family used to celebrate the *holi* festival of the Hindus for several days on end in the famous garden of Moti Jhil. Nawab Sirajuddowla and Mirjafar also used to attend these festivals.

The architecture of Bengal during the Musim period is a remarkable evidence of how the Hindu styles combined with the Saracenic to produce a new form of the building art, considered by authorities on architecture to be peculiar to Bengal. Art-historians have shown that the craftsmen of the mosques and tombs of Gauda, Pandua and Malda were most of them Hindus who almost invariably adapted their own technique to the needs of their Muslim masters. It is well-known that the Hindus of Bengal developed a wonderful terra-cotta art and fine-moulded ornamental brick-work which they employed lavishly in their temples. The following are a few instances of the influence that these as well as other crafts of the Hindus exerted on the Muslim buildings of the medieval age.

It is believed that the art of enamelling tiles and bricks, so much in evidence in the Muslim buildings in India was a local art in Gauda. The designs on the brick-built *liwan* of the famous Sona Masjid (sixteenth century) at Gauda are adaptations from the Hindu terra-cotta work. The door-ways of this mosque with cusped Hindu arches, and their frames of carved architraves are similar to those of Hindu shrines. The stone-pillars in it are of a distinctly Hindu origin, as also its curved cornices and the vaulted side aisles imitative of the ancient bamboo roofing of Bengal. The domes of the Jami Masjid retain their Hindu finales. If the motifs of the decoration in the Muslim buildings are of Hindu origin and similar to the indigenous terra-cotta work of Bengal, the Saracenic influence on them is the exquisite calligraphic work done by the Arabic and Persian artists. The beautiful *mihrab* of the Adinah mosque (fourteenth century) at Gauda is so obviously Hindu in design as hardly to require comment. The outer arch of it looks like the trefoil arched canopy of the image of Vishnu, found in the Manbhum district, but the inscriptions and arabesque ornament in it are, undoubtedly, contributions of Saracenic art. These Muslim buildings considerably influenced the construction of many Hindu temples of later times of which a notable example is the temple at Kantanagar in the Dinajpur district which was built early in the eighteenth century after the style of the mosques at Gauda and Malda.

The growth of cultural fellowship in Bengal during the mediaeval times, as outlined above, was not however an accident or a chance phenomenon. It was an expression of the assimilative genius of the race, and it represented a stage, full of meaning, of the journey towards the goal. The art, literature and religion, even the social and political life of the period, furnish, as we have seen, striking proofs of how the various communities in Bengal were tending to open out into a common cultural consciousness. Things, however, could not take any definite form in as much as conditions in the external life of the country were not always favourable. Neither had the country before it a clear vision of the synthesis that was destined to come to it in the future.

TOWARDS A LARGER FELLOWSHIP

The modern age dawned in India under conditions that were anything but happy. Indeed, the immediate reactions of the impact of Europe on India seemed for a time to be disruptive of her own culture and civilisation, but that was not to endure. This dynamic foreign influence had certainly a secret purpose to fulfil in the plan of Nature for preparing India to attain her ultimate goal. The intelligentsia of Bengal, who were the first to imbibe it, found themselves infected with all that was coarse and unhealthy in it and failed at the outest to appreciate and accept its finer and more life-giving elements. But Bengal, it must be said to her credit, did not take long to get over this infection and show signs of a resurgence, which were nowhere more marked than in the spiritual endeavours of the race; for, it is, as always, by these only that India can rediscover her soul. To stem the tide of a hedonistic Europeanism was not, therefore, the only aim of the movements that rose and flourished in Bengal and then swept over the rest of India. Nature's aim in them was to prepare the country for a greater future, a nobler destiny. "Bengal thus became the first workshop of the Shakti of India."[1] It was she who was chosen by the Mother to nurse and give form

[1] Sri Aurobindo, *The Renaissance in India*, p. 60.

to the forces released by her for resuscitating the national life of the country, for re-affirming to her children the ideals that were their imperishable heritage from a magnificent past.

Harmony as the truth, Freedom as the means, and Perfection as the end, have more than once come to the vision of India, and this time they dawned upon the vision of those pioneer-souls who had made their advent in Bengal during the nineteenth century, verily as the instruments of the Mother for the accomplishment of her work in India. They became the acknowledged inaugurators of a new epoch in which the renascent soul of India broke into those expressions which were to advance the progress of the race beyond any conceivable bounds. Because of their intuitive seeing of a cosmic order of things, everything these leaders said or did bore the stamp of a catholic outlook, so gloriously incarnated by the movements that go by their names. It is proposed here to give a brief account of how in her creative activities, Bengal opened her heart and enlarged it, so as to deepen and extend her fellowship with others, a fellowship that she had been trying to build up through the ages.

I

Notwithstanding the vicissitudes through which the country passed during the eighteenth century, it cannot be said that there was any dearth of friendly relations between the communities that made Bengal what she then was. The *tols* of old continued as citadels of orthodox Brahminism attracting scholars from different parts of India, who would flock to them for the study, among other things, of the *Navya-Nyāya*—the new system of Logic,—and of the *Gaudiya-riti*—Bengal's own style of Sanskrit composition,—for both of which she was famous all over India. On the other hand, there were the *maktābs* where devout Muslims were expounding the tenets of Islam, and were helping the more liberal among the Hindus to learn Arabic and Persian, which they had been accustomed to do for centuries. Some of these Hindus were noted for their original composition in those languages. Mention may be made of Poet Bhâratchandra and Raja Rammohan Roy. The Persian poems of the former were no less a credit to him than his Bengali ones. And the latter chose Persian and Arabic for discussing some of his important views on religion. There were other evidences to show that cultural fellowship was fostered by the Hindus and Muslims alike. The court of Maharaja Krishnachandra was adorned by famous writers from both the communities. The Muslim Fakir was no less popular among the Hindus than before. The various cults, derived from Tantricism, Buddhism and Vaishnavism, described in the previous chapter, kept on drawing to their folds more and more adherents from all castes and creeds, thereby breaking the barriers that separated them. The most renowned Tantric of the time was Ramprasad, the 'child of the Mother', in whom we find a wonderful combination of an ecstatic Vaishnavic devotion with a direct intuition of the all-ruling presence of the Shakti. He gave his whole mind and heart to the Mother, and as a response to his intense and insistent call She revealed Herself to him in one of Her supreme forms. His songs which were the fire-surge of his exalted soul have immortalised him in the heart of Bengal. Indeed, they seem to be the impassioned outpourings of Bengal's own soul. Alike to the Hindu and Muslim devotees of Kali, they are, as ever, the very *mantram* of their worship. The story goes that once while going in his boat on the river Hooghly Sirajuddowla heard Ramprasad singing, as he was having his bath in the river. The Nawab was so much impressed that he invited Ramprasad to his boat and asked him to sing the same song and not one in Hindi which Ramprasad was trying to do, thinking that the Nawab might not be able to follow his Bengali. Even with the proselytizing Christians the relations of the Hindus were no less happy. It was Ramram Bose, a Hindu, who composed the earliest Bengali hymns for the Christian church, and this without losing faith in his own religion in the least. This was typical of the spirit of old Bengal.

The above activities, however, do not give an adequate idea of the state of Bengal before this period of transition had set in. Stuck in the mire of her old ways, she was slowly sinking into a state of stagnation, if not of decline. There was no new horizon looming before her, no fresh outlet for her dormant energy. A liberation from such an impasse was her crying need. The onslaught from the West provided the necessary condition that compelled the race to wake up and make an effort to find its own self. Raja Rammohan Roy was chosen by the Mother to embody this great impulse, and be the first resounding voice of a new national aspiration. A pioneer and torchbearer, the Raja stood head and shoulders above his countrymen and gave a lead which helped not only to counteract the evils, rampant everywhere, but also opened their eyes to a new vision of freedom and harmony. His emotional Bengali heart welled up in a surge of love for his motherland. But this love did not in any way narrow down the outlook of this great man. He had a rare mastery of the teachings of all the religions of the world, and he realised fully that all religions are but different ways of looking at the one selfsame truth of this world. The growth of this wide outlook in him was not a little due to the Tantric discipline he had gone through and to his study of the sublime Upanishadic literature. It was not without meaning that Rammohan endeavoured to establish Mahanirvan Tantra as the Scripture of the Brahmo Samaj. The formulae and forms of the Samaj were borrowed from the Tantra. If. later, the orthodox members of it abandoned these Tantric ideas, many among them even now recite the Hymn to the Brahman which occurs in the Mahanirvan Tantra.

Rammohan's idea of religious universalism was but the flowering out in him of the genius of his race. The interfusion of cults that had been taking place in Bengal throughout is an idea of the innate synthetic tendency of her mind. And Rammohan certainly showed that tendency when he founded the Brahmo Samaj as a Society of the worshippers of the one God of all religions and all humanity. The Samaj was to be a place of public meeting for all men without distinctions, a place where all can join in a common worship and adoration of the one and only God. The worshippers might belong each to his own religion and yet join in religious communion with the votaries of other faiths in order that such common worship and prayer might strengthen all and help the world to move more surely and more truly towards the centre of the universe, the one Eternal and Immutable Being. This in modern times was the very first call on India to awaken to the truth of the Spirit which is the essential aim of all religions, but which they have not always cared to emphasise. And this was a more express attempt to widen the sphere of that spiritual fellowship of which the foundation had been laid by the

Tantrics, the Buddhists and the Vaishnavas of old Bengal.

Rammohan's exposition of the Upanishads and the Vedanta ranked him as a Hindu of Hindus, typically Brahminical; his interpretation of the *Shariat* and the *Hadis* made the Muslims think that he was one of their faith; and his arguments for Unitarian Christianity were taken to be those of a Christian rationalist. Such was the characteristic expression of a soul that understood the essential unity of all religions in the Lord. The spiritual influence of the Brahmo Samaj movement has been more subtle than apparent. It was, however, perceptible in the turn that the educated Indian mind took towards the higher values of life, towards the spiritual treasures of their own country. Moreover, the educational and social reforms that this movement originated and inspired were the great starting-point of all that was done along these lines in later times. The Raja was the prime mover in so many directions! His famous letter to the Minister of Foreign Affairs in France revealed him as the first champion of International Fellowship in modern times. All these ideas and activities as well as those that came after them broadened the outlook of the Indian people, freed and led their minds into those fresh undertakings which culminated in a wonderful renaissance, incomparable in modern history. It is through them, indeed, that the Shakti of India has been preparing the country for the greater future to which it is destined. And there is no gainsaying the fact that they helped to enlarge the tradition of cultural fraternity which it has been given to Bengal to foster through the ages as the very basis of all the higher endeavours of the race.

Whatever he was in his inner life—and a wide complex personality like his always baffles analysis—Rammohan's outstanding public work exhibited his Vedantic inclinations. It was from the Brahmo Samaj thought that Bengal received her first initiation into Vedanta in modern times, and thereby revived her sense of oneness with the whole of India. Indeed, Bengal needed it, needed the discipline of knowledge, so as to grow in readiness for the vaster synthesis of the future.

But the movement could not keep to the original intention of the founder. Its mind became more active than its heart; and it was betrayed into a dryness of mere intellectualism making it necessary for the heart of Bengal to rise and take the field and give a lead. Keshab Chandra Sen was the next man to fulfil that need. He developed his Vaishnavic ardour through his contact with the great Bejoy Krishna Goswami; and his adoration of the Mother was intensified by his association with Sri Ramakrishna. His passionate cries like "Oh Thou Mother Divine! bind me with Thy mercies", may be mistaken for those of Ramprasad or Sri Ramakrishna. Many of his songs and sayings, as also his love for congregational chant (*kirtan*), express the emotions of *bhakti* that surged in his heart. On the day Keshab laid the foundation of his Church of New Dispensation, a big Sankirtan party went round the streets of Calcutta singing the memorable song:

"To grant salvation the merciful God has sent his new faith of Brahmoism. Lo! the gates of salvation are wide open; He calls one and all; entrance through His gate is free; no one ever returns disappointed; the rich and the poor, the wise and the ignorant, all are equally welcome there.

"Men and women of all classes have an equal right: whoever truly loves God. the same shall be saved, there is no caste distinction here."

The voice of Keshab combined the profound messages of the East and the West, and it accentuated the essential unity of the spiritual experiences of all countries. It was under his direction that the first complete translation of the Koran (with commentaries) from the original Arabic into Bengali was prepared and published. His admiration for Christ and his teachings was construed by many as a virtual profession of Christianity. Keshab was undoubtedly an eclectic and a reconciler. In whatever he said or did he was inspired by the fervent longing of his soul to establish peace and harmony, broadbased on the underlying unity of things. He believed that harmony would come for ever to this earth only when mankind was united in a common spiritual seeking.

II

But the Brahmo Samaj movement, even the *bhakti* aspect of it under Keshab's leadership, could not extend its hold beyond the pale of the educated sections of India, although its influences were all the time and are even now, working to elevate the social and cultural life of the whole country. The new knowledge from the West was spreading fast. It had to be acquired and assimilated into the being of the race. And that could not be done so long as the race did not have a complete understanding of its own self. The Mother, therefore, manifested Herself before her chosen child Sri Ramakrishna, and gave him the strength to uphold the ideals of India by living them in his own life. Indeed, Sri Ramakrishna is the first in modern times to build on the sure foundation of a direct vision of the Divine. He saw the Para Brahman of the Vedanta, and also the Para-Shakti of the Tantras; and he saw them in the infinity of the One Reality,—a realisation so important to the work that he had come to accomplish. He pursued one after another, and with the avidity of a neophyte, the three great forms of spiritual discipline evolved in India, and even practised the two other living religions of the world. And in every one of them he won such unique victories as no seeker before him had achieved in a single life. His heroic march along the most dangerous of the paths—that of the Tantras—gave him wonderful visions, sublimating experiences, and ultimately, the supreme realisation of the Transcendent Mahâ-Shakti. He saw the mystery of creation unfolded before him. He heard the music of the inner worlds, their rhythms and symphonies. He mastered the secrets of the supernatural powers. And he came out bright as gold, possessing spiritual knowledge of a very high order. The Vaishnavic discipline found in him a most devoted adherent. An absolute love for Krishna made him mad. And he approached Him through all the *bhâvas* (attitudes) to which He responds. He became a Gopi brimming over with ecstatic emotions, and took part in the mystic *lilâ* with the divine Sweetheart. Seized by the *mahâbhâva* of Râdhâ he became identified with her and the blissful fulfilment of his *sâdhanâ* was when Krishna appeared before him and merged in his person. The next was his gigantic conquest in the Advaita practice, which he achieved by realising his identity with the Para-Brahman, the Absolute Existence, Consciousness and Bliss. "The soul was lost in the Self. Dualism was blotted out. Beyond word and beyond thought, he attained Brahman." And he achieved in a single day what had taken even his own spiritual guide no less than forty years. Sri Ramkrishna remained in that state for six whole months.—a veritable miracle.

This realisation as well as those he had had before made him a master of Hindu spiritual disciplines. He felt impelled to seek the experiences that other religions had to offer. It was indeed utterly daring of him—a Brahmin by caste and a priest—to have formally got initiated into Islam. He followed its customs like an orthodox Muslim, repeating the name of *Allah* and performing his *namaz* regularly. In only three days he had a vision of the Prophet, and in no time realised the formless God of the Koran, only to find himself identified with the Brahman, the goal already attained by him through his Advaitic practice. Years after, Sri Ramakrishna wanted to know the truth of Christianity. He first made himself acquainted with the teachings of Christ, and one day as he was looking at a picture of Madonna he felt overwhelmed by the descent into him of a downpour of heavenly effulgence radiated by the picture. The Hindu Brahmin was now a follower of Christ. For three days he thought of nothing but Christ. On the fourth day the Son of Man appeared before the child of the Divine Mother and took the latter into his bosom and became one with him. Christ merged in Ramakrishna and he had an immediate experience of Brahman with attributes. Sri Ramakrishna's love for the Buddha requires no recapitulation. He regarded the Tathâgata and the Christ as incarnations of God. And the Advaitic realisation does not differ much from the Nirvanic.

This is how Sri Ramakrishna for the first time in the spiritual history of mankind realised and proclaimed the harmony, nay the unity, of all religions the vision of which had come to him out of a direct and intuitive seeing of the One Reality in Its many aspects. And it is this harmony for which Bengal has been striving through the ages, because it is this that is to be the basis for the still greater achievements of the race in times to come.

Sri Ramakrishna's was a call upon man to wake up and turn towards God the Mother—that is how he called Him—not because He is the God of any particular religion but because He is the one God of all religions the one source of unity and harmony. There can indeed be no surer foundation for human fellowship than this great truth which was lived and vindicated by the God-man of Dakshineswar. The Personal and the Impersonal aspects of the Supreme, even the paths of knowledge and devotion have been difficult for many seekers to reconcile. But in the higher experience of Sri Ramakrishna they lost their separateness. In his own words: "The Personal and the Impersonal are the same Being, like milk and its whiteness, or the diamond and its lustre, or the serpent and its sinuosity. It is impossible to conceive of the one without the other. The Divine Mother and Brahman are one." But he was always a child of the Mother. It was she in whom he lived, moved and had his being. He was in constant communion with her. He did nothing without Her sanction. He felt Her presence everywhere and in everything. He saw Her light in man, and saw the oneness of all humanity in the luminous world of the Mother. To awaken man to that light and thereby help him prepare for a greater life was the work for which the Mother had brought Ramakrishna back to his physical consciousness from the state of trance in the transcendental region of the Absolute in which he had remained for six long months. The magic spell of his contact soon began to spread. The intellectuals, the Europeanised Indians or the orthodox pundits, who came to argue, remained to pray at the feet of this God-drunk unlettered Brahmin, captivated by his matchless wisdom and mastery of spiritual things. Even the guides who had been with him to help in his spiritual practices stayed on to imbibe more and more of the divine exhalations of his unique personality which, as well as the universal character of his teachings, attracted people of all castes and sects who wended their way from far and near to the holy shrine of Dakshineswar. Indeed, to see and hear him was to be exalted in mind and heart and soul. Thus began a new era of spiritual fellowship, of which Sri Ramakrishna was the God-appointed inaugurator. But who was to proclaim to the world the message of the

Master? Who was to be the apostle and exponent of his lofty teachings and the hero of action to make those teachings dynamic in the life of the nation and forge fresh links of a spiritual-cultural fellowship for the collective well-being of humanity? The Master himself prepared one for that work by pouring into him whatever strength he had. That one was Vivekananda.

Therefore that mighty son of India, made all the more mighty by his Guru's grace, thundered out to the world the central message of the Vedanta "Thou art That". Never before was there one who had spoken of the divinity of man with such an electrifying intensity of conviction as that soldier of the Light, that heaven-born hierophant of God. His was a soul of fire which was all the time burning to cast abroad the truths he had been taught by his Master, the truths he himself had gained by his amazing *tapasyā*. And were they not the same truths that India has preserved through the ages, so that they might be disseminated once again for the spiritual uplift of mankind? And was not Vivekananda their greatest exponent who won for India a glory that cannot be compared to anything of its kind in modern times?

Vivekananda believed that man had inherent in him his own perfection, and that, to manifest it was the sole purpose of his existence. Nay, he saw in man the Brahman and like the Rishi in the Upanishad addressed the whole of humanity as the children of immortal bliss. He realised the oneness of all religious experiences like his Master and declared: "I accept all religions that were in the past and worship them all. I worship God with everyone of them, in whatever form they worship Him. I shall go to the mosque of a Muhammadan, I shall enter the Christian church and kneel before the Crucifix; I shall enter the Buddhist temple, where I shall take refuge in Buddha and his Law. I shall go into the forest and sit down in meditation with the Hindu, who is trying to see the light which enlightens the heart of everyone. Not only shall I do all these, I shall keep my heart open for all that may come in the future.... The Bible, the Vedas, the Koran and all other sacred books are so many pages, and an infinite number of pages remain yet to be unfolded. I would leave my heart open for all of them." Once he told an American audience that he had come not to convert them into Hinduism but to make them better Christians.

Yet his luminous interpretation of the Vedantic standpoint in spirituality attracted seekers from every part of the world, who formed the first nucleus of a world-fellowship based on the intrinsic unity of man in the Spirit. Whether it was America or England or the Continent, wherever he went, people of all classes flocked to him only to be illumined in their soul by a new light. Spiritual India, reawakened after a long sleep, spoke through him her message of the divine heritage of man; and the materialistic West bowed its head before the majesty and sublimity of that message. The holy land of the Mother became thus a place of pilgrimage for many of those children of Europe who came in contact with the Swami's magnetic personality. One of those who were fired by his spiritual idealism was that wonderful woman, Sister Nivedita, who made India her home and lived and worked for her with a rare devotion and an unparalleled insight into Indian culture and thought. It was a new form of cultural confraternity that grew under the dynamic influence of Vivekananda. It showed how a true, inner understanding of India could promote an intimate relation with her. "This time India is to be centre of a world-wide spiritual awakening", said the great Swami. Those, therefore, who were to prepare themselves for it must know what India truly was. Hence began the steady influx into India of her admirers and devotees from distant countries, who wanted to join with her children in a common endeavour to drink at the fountain of eternal wisdom discovered by the fathers of the race. It is a response to the call of human fellowship that India had ever extended to the world.

Vivekananda thought that in order to be the harbinger of that new age of the Spirit, India must herself be great again in her soul. She must regain possession of her inner riches. She must revision the past in its true perspective and cull from it whatever was likely to contribute to the re-creation of her future. The Swami proclaimed his prophetic vision thus: "The fiat has gone forth, India must rise." "None can resist her more; never is she going to sleep any more; no outward powers can hold her back any more; for the infinite giant is rising to her feet." His command was: "Our children must know from their very birth that their lives are dedicated to their motherland." And the first thing for them to do is to know what exactly is the soul of India, the source of her vitality. The fiery words of the Swami were: "When the life-blood is strong and pure, no disease germ can live in the body. Our life-blood is spirituality. If it flows clear, pure and vigorous, everything is right; political, social, any other material defect, even the poverty of the land will be all cured if that blood is pure." "The banner of the spiritual cannot be raised too high in this country. In it alone is salvation."

Renunciation of ego, service of God in man, love of humanity, establishment of peace on earth, and the discovery of harmony in everything, were the high aims with which Vivekananda founded the Math and the Mission in the name of his Master. They have since grown and expanded into an immense network of organisations of social and spiritual service spread all over the world. It is in these centres that seekers of all castes, creeds and races congregate and share a common life of inner quest. But Vivekananda's influence has even been something much deeper and wider. Here, there and everywhere he still lives amongst us as a subtle elevating force, an inextinguishable fire which it is difficult not to be caught by. In the words of Sri Aurobindo: "We perceive his influence still working gigantically, we know not well how, we know not well where, in something that is not yet formed, something leonine, grand, intuitive, upheaving that has entered the soul of India and we say, 'Behold, Vivekananda still lives in the soul of his Mother and in the souls of her children'."[1] This is how that mighty son of India sowed the seeds of a larger fellowship in the hearts of her children. His was not, just as they never were either Rammohan's or Keshab's or Ramakrishna's, a narrow creed, a cramped religious or social dogma, a petty exclusive patriotism. He represented all that is radiantly noble and large and universal, all that is harmonious and beautiful and beneficently robust and powerful in man. He stood for the service of God in man, irrespective of all outer denominational distinctions. His soul knew a boundless embrace and his wide heart bled—literally bled—for all who were poor and lowly, depressed and distressed. What loftier strains of spiritual humanism have ever been heard, what surer foundations of human solidarity and fellowship

[1] Sri Aurobindo, *Bankim-Tilak-Dayananda*, p. 49.

ever laid in this, our world of mutual hates and animosities, of mean parochial interests and bigoted individual and communal rivalries than in the following words of the Swami? "I have lost all wish for my salvation; may I be born again and again and suffer thousands of miseries so that I may worship the only God that exists, the only God I believe in, the sum-total of all souls,—and above all my God the wicked, my God the miserable, my God the poor of all races, of all species is the special object of my worship. He who is the high and the low, the saint and the sinner, the god and the worm, His worship, the visible, the knowable, the real, the omnipresent; break all other idols. In whom there is neither past life nor future birth, nor death nor going nor coming, in whom we always have been and always will be one, Him worship; break all other idols."

III

Almost immediately after Vivekananda's passing away, Bengal, as if by a galvanic shock, leapt into a new impulse and expressed it in the outburst of 1905. The immediate cause of it, however, was only an occasion for the Mother to reveal Herself to her children and inspire them to dedicate themselves at the altar of their country's freedom. Whatever might have been the way or ways in which they responded to this call, the fact is there that they made a passionate endeavour to liberate their motherland from the foreign yoke. Besides, there was a deeper intention in all that they did. They wanted the freedom of India not that she might develop and prosper materially only, but that she might be great again in the Spirit so as to be able to deliver her message to humanity and lead it to its divine goal. And to that end they were stirred by the mantra which Bankimchandra, the prophet of spiritual patriotism, saw and uttered in a rare moment of inspiration. Bankim gave through *Bande Mātaram* the vision of the Mother, the Shakti of India, that was vouchsafed to him, and "in a single day a whole people had been converted to the religion of patriotism."[1] It is by this mantra that Bengal worshipped the Mother and invoked her strength to go forth and conquer. It is by the magic of this word that the entire race was fired into a common seeking and a common striving. Hindus and Muslims uttered it in one voice, and they did so with all the depth and intensity of their soul. Even Hindus were moved to tears when that intrepid patriot, Maulvi Liakat Hussain, would cry out this national mantra and go on repeating it so many times over again. Soon it set ablaze the whole of the country and gave it a foretaste of liberty. Thus, the fellowship for the attainment of a common goal, into which Bengal was

[1] Sri Aurobindo, *Bankim-Tilak-Dayananda*, p. 14.

united by this mantra, began to grow all over India, fostered by the force of the word itself. The children of the Mother uttered it only to be caught by its animating spell. And in that cry of the soul, the oneness and unity of India became articulate once again.

But the movement was not a mere political one. There was a spiritual side to it; as, in a sense, it incarnated the true renascent spirit of Bengal. The cult of Shakti is the cult of her soul. It flowed as an unfailing sap and sustenance in all Rammohan's giant undertakings, it assumed a more vibrant, if somewhat vague and indefinite expression in Keshab, and then in Sri Ramakrishna it blazed forth into a splendour of creative and constructive power. Vivekananda, though a Vedantin in his soul, had his heart full of the Mother, and whatever he did was by the strength of Kali that his Master had instilled into him. The youths of Bengal adored the same Shakti, first, in the form of their own land, then in the image of India, regarding Her as the conscious emanation of the Divine Mother; and when She revealed herself to them, they consecrated themselves at her feet and did what they thought would bring about the realisation of India's destiny. Indeed, they saw the Mother, so vividly described by Bankim, the Mother as she was in the glorious past, as she is in the sorrowful present, and as she will be in the more glorious future. This sharing of a common vision of the

Mother by a whole people was undoubtedly a step forward on the path to a larger fellowship in the future. That there was a divine guidance behind the movement was the intuition of one who saw far into the depth of things and declared: "Nationalism is a religion that has come to India from God"[1] and that "there is a great Power at work to help India; and we are doing what it bids us".[2] It is in this vision of Bengal that lies the inward meaning of the movement of 1905. And it is this again that must be understood if a correct estimate is to be made of what Bengal did to advance the political progress of India.

Most of those who were connected with the leadership of this movement were themselves earnest seekers of God, disciples of well-known spiritual leaders of the time, and were endowed with an insight into the soul of India. Each of them was a veritable dynamo of force and inspiration, burning with a whole-hearted love for his motherland. The youths of Bengal gathered round them, caught the contagion of that love, left their hearths and homes and went out in quest of the Mother. What these leaders said and wrote about the culture and civilisation of the 'Eternal and Timeless India', about her problems and the ways in which they were to be approached and solved created a wonderful literature which put its indelible stamp on the mind of the people.

[1] Speeches of Aurobindo Ghose, p 10
[2] *Ibid*, p 32.

Indeed, the *Bande Mátaram*, the *Karmayogin*, the many Bengali journals—were no mere periodicals but living evangels of profound truths that ennoble and exalt, guide and mould. These writings helped in the growth of a comman national consciousness, and made the people realise that they were one in the indivisible unity of India and that the solution of her problems must be attempted by all of them together. And as this feeling deepened in them they began to be more and more united in their striving towards the attainment of their common goal,—the re-enthronement of the Mother in her own temple. And where can that temple be but in the hearts of her children?

Nor was this awakening confined to spiritual and political spheres only. Its breath blew through the creations of the artistic and literary genius of the race, the former achieving at one bound, as it were, a startling originality and depth of self-expression in the works of the Bengal painters, and the latter uttering itself in the ocean-roll of Bankim's prose and the dreamy dissolving music and mystic lyricism of Tagore's poetry. Bankim was the seer-prophet of the new awakening and in his writings he made a vigorous attempt to recapture the ancient ideals of the race and restate them from a rationalistic standpoint. Tagore was the master-singer of the age. But both of them, besides being fathers of a literature of matchless excellence, were the fore-runners of the greater era that was to come in the future. "Both show an increasing return to the Indian spirit in fresh forms; both are the voices of the dawn, seek more than they find, suggest and are calling for more than they evoke."[1] "The poetry of Tagore owes its sudden and universal success to this advantage that he gives us more of this discovery and fusion (of the truth and reality of the spirit in man and in things and the insistence on life) of which the mind of our age is in quest than any other creative writer of the time. His work is a constant music of the overpassing of the borders, a chant-filled realm in which the subtle sounds and lights of the spirit give new meanings to the finer subtleties of life."[2] It was this vision of his by which Tagore was able to interpret in forms of surpassing beauty the abiding truths of the past of India. Nature chose him as the one man in history to receive for his poetry the unstinted homage of the whole of mankind during his lifetime. The poet of India became the poet of the world,—a fact which has certainly helped forward the cause of India's cultural fellowship with humanity, to the growth of which the substantial contribution of the Bengal artists also deserves an honourable mention. These pioneer-artists tried almost with immediate success to give a visual expression to the immortal spirit of India. They revived the splendid traditions of the ancient

---

[1] Sri Aurobindo, *The Renaissance in India*, p. 65.

[2] Sri Aurobindo in *Arya*, vol. VI, p. 440.

masters, and their works reflect the aesthetic genius of the race. "The whole power of the Bengal artists springs from their deliberate choice of the spirit and hidden meaning in things rather than their form and surface meaning as the object to be expressed. It is intuitive and its forms are the very rhythm of its intuition, they have little to do with the metric formalities devised by the observing intellect; it leans over the finite to discover its suggestions of the infinite and inexpressible; it turns to outward life and nature to found upon it lines and colours, rhythms and embodiments which will be significant of the other life and other nature than the physical which all that is merely outward conceals. This is the eternal motive of Indian art."[1] Art-historians are of opinion that the Ajanta masters, at least some of them, were Bengalis. The influence of Ajanta on the neo-Bengal School of Painting, of which Abanindranath Tagore is the founder, might be taken to be a return of the race to its old aesthetic intuition. Students of this School are now at the head of many art-institutions in India. Its works have received the best of praises everywhere in the world. On seeing the famous painting "Buddha carrying the kid" by Nandalal Bose, shown in an exihibition at Geneva, a Swiss critic remarked: "I see behind this picture a great civilisation." The contributions of Sister Nivedita

[1] *The Renaissance in India*, p. 62.

and E. B. Havell to the growth of this School shall never be forgotten. Their interpretation of India's art and cultural history is as deep as it is illuminating.

There was yet another aspect of this awakening. A nation cannot progress without a sound system of education. The ideals of the race, as rediscovered by its modern seers, had to be inculcated upon the youths. The foreign system of education, then in vogue, being found inadequate to meet the demands of an enlarging life and thought, it was felt that a system must be evolved which would take into account the innate inclinations of the people, its own culture and traditions. Endeavours began, therefore, to be made in that direction, and these, like the literary and spiritual, were gaining ground before the actual manifestation of the new spirit in the political sphere. Indeed, Rammohan, Keshab and Vivekananda, had each his own ideas about the ways in which the training of the young should be devised. And they made some beginnings, too, towards the materialisation of those ideas. The later leaders of the country had also their schemes and plans which they tried to carry out with much boldness and enthusiasm; and their work was not without its lesson for the future reconstruction of the nation.

Poet Tagore, however, gave in his own way a new form to this impulse. He realised the utter hollowness of the existing educational system and started at Santiniketan a school—unique of its kind—where in an atmosphere of freedom, joy, peace and beauty of Nature children might be helped to grow into the fullness of their personalities. With this school as the nucleus was undertaken that far-sighted educational venture which was to develop into an international university. The terrible devastation caused by the Great War of 1914 moved the Poet into thinking that the study and appreciation of each other's culture might promote mutual understanding among the nations and pave the way to a deeper unity in the collective life of mankind. He, therefore, rechristened his school into Visva-Bharati with the express object of helping "East and West to meet there in a common fellowship of study, and thereby ultimately to strengthen the fundamental condition of world-peace through the establishment of free communication of ideas between the two hemispheres. It is to be a centre of Culture where research into and study of the religion, literature, history, science, and art of Hindu, Buddhist, Jaina, Islamic, Sikh, Christian and other cultures of Asia may be pursued along with the culture of the West, with that simplicity in externals which is necessary for true spiritual realisation, in amity, good fellowship and co-operation between the thinkers and scholars of both Eastern and Western countries, free from antagonism of race, nationality, creed or caste, and in the name of the One Supreme Being who is

Shantam, Shivam, Advaitam."[1] Explaining the name the Poet wrote in Sanskrit: *"yatra visvam bhavaty eka-nidam"* (where the whole world finds its common shelter). "Visva-Bharati," in the words of the Poet again, "represents India where she has her wealth of mind which is for all. Visva-Bharati acknowledges India's obligation to offer to others the hospitality of her best culture and India's right to accept from others their best. It is India's invitation to the world, her offer of sacrifice to the highest truth of man."[2]

Eminent scholars and indologists of all countries, deeply impressed by this noble ideal and by the sincerity with which it was proclaimed, began to pour in along with a constant stream of students, visitors and visiting professors, who passed months and years at Visva-Bharati in pursuit of their respective subjects for which proper facilities were made available. They lived there a common corporate life and by sharing its simplicities with Indians imbibed more and more of the Indian spirit. Not to speak of those two noble-hearted Englishmen, Wyllie Pearson and Charlie Andrews, who expressed their love for Tagore and his country by making Santiniketan their home, world-famous orientalists like Sylvain Levi of France, Mark Winternitz of Czecho-Slovakia, Sten Konow of Norway, Carlo Formichi of Italy, Julius Germanus of Hungary, James

[1] Visva-Bharati Bulletin No. 12.
[2] *Ibid.*

Pratt of America, and Poure-a-Davoud of Persia, responded to the call of Visva-Bharati. These as well as scholars from Europe and America, from different parts of India and Asia, from Tibet, China, Japan, Indonesia, Ceylon, Burma have by their adherence to a common ideal built up at Santiniketan a new tradition of cultural fellowship that will go down in history as a unique phenomenon of international confraternity in the world of creative research. The eminent Chinese savant Tan Yun-Shan, the Founder-Director of the Sino-Indian Cultural Society, became the Poet's collaborator in starting the Chinese section of Visva-Bharati, which now possesses a fine hall and a Chinese library, the biggest in the whole world outside China, where Chinese and Indian scholars are exploring literary evidences of the old cultural bonds between their countries. Indeed, to renew this friendship has for many years been the chief mission of Prof. Tan; and he believes with all his heart that the new world of freedom and peace will come into being through the joint efforts of China and India.

But research is not the only activity of Visva-Bharati. Its academic and art sections promote cultural fellowship no less remarkably. They also attract students from different parts of India and even from abroad. By participating in a common quest of knowledge and beauty, these learners help the growth of a confraternity which is an outstanding feature of the institution. A new School of Art has developed there under the guidance of Nandalal Bose. The impressions that Nandalal had of the art of China and other countries when he visited them have been absorbed by him into the native genius of his own art so much so that when they emerge into expression in his work they bear the distinctive stamp of the artist's own originality. The work of Nandalal and largely that of his School is marked by power, freedom and clarity. Many Art Schools in India are in the charge of the successful students of Visva-Bharati. In dancing, new forms have been evolved out of a blending of the existing Indian and Oriental styles. In music also many new turns have been given to the old techniques. The work of the Visva-Bharati for the reclamation of the neighbouring villages has revived the old spirit of co-operation on which all the glory of rural India was built. This is how the educational venture of Tagore offers to the world its greatest gift, a marvellous ideal of cultural fellowship. Indeed, Visva-Bharati is to the Bengal of to-day what Nalanda was to her in the past.

Bengal has been ever open to all wholesome influences from outside. The impact of the West quickened her into the discovery of her own self and its immense powers and potentialities; and as she discovered them, she began to receive into her own being new ideas from Europe and adapt them to the creation of fresh forms in the world of her life and culture. This process could be perceived in her social and political life, in her literary efforts, but more prominently in her scientific undertakings to which she, with the rest of India, was largely inspired by Europe. The discoveries of Jagadish Chandra Bose are a colossal contribution by an Indian mind in the domain of Science. Starting from the conceptions of Western Science Jagadish Chandra went beyond their scope and saw in inert Matter essentially the same pulsation of life as is more clearly discernible in the animal. It was a secret that Nature, the Mother of things, revealed to a son of Bengal. The work of other well-known scientists of Bengal is also considerable. Science, therefore, no less than art, has proved to be another cohesive factor in the cultural fellowship of India, and of the world in general. And when we look at the developing language and literature of Bengal we find a most tangible testimony of her contact with many cultures. It has been enriched by elements from almost all the major languages of India, and of countries far beyond her borders. All these elements the Bengali language has absorbed into its own body and it has become in the hands of its modern makers one of the most progressive languages of the world.

But this power of assimilation Bengal seems to-day to have lost to some extent, because of her tendency—a deplorable tendency—to deviate from her own line of development. The ideals for which India has stood through the ages, and which her sons have so gloriously vindicated in her recent past, appear to-day to be dimmed, if not covered over by extrinsic influences, in her national consciousness. The leaders of the movements subsequent to the first uprising of 1905 have not cared to re-affirm India's own ideals to the country, far less to indicate the path towards their attainment. These movements have more or less proceeded along Western lines under a very thin disguise, and having no roots in the undying spirit of the race. The result is that Bengal in her collective life stands to-day arrested in her advance, undecided and hesitant. Dazed by the glamour of imported ideas, beset with forces of disintegration, she presents the pitiable picture of a perplexed, self-divided derelict. Will materialism save and satisfy her soul? Will economics or politics, however sound or humane, restore her to her ancient greatness? Will an ethical ideal redeem and exalt her? None of these means are likely to avail, for they all have their birth in the dim ignorance of a seeking mind, not in the steady light of true knowledge. It is only by turning to her soul, by unsealing the perennial well-spring of her own spiritual powers, by recreating herself from within, by receiving light from beyond the frontiers of her groping mind that she can rise to her full stature and assume her destined role in the new world of tomorrow.

A decisive turn inward, an intense spiritual

seeking, is, therefore, the crying need. Spirituality —a virile, conquering and dynamic spirituality— is the only solution. If it is to be great again, the race must rekindle its inherent aspiration towards the Spirit. That inner fire must flame up again. All cultural upheavals in India have always been inspired by this dominant urge of her soul. Culture is that which prepares man for a greater life. And true fellowship is that which makes man realise his unity with others in a common effort to achieve that end. But fellowship acquires its highest meaning when it is not only enlarged but also deepened, so that it might be an integration of awakened souls towards the building up of a perfect community which can come into being only through the collective growth of man into a higher consciousness, a diviner nature.

It has already been shown how in her past Bengal has gone through the various spiritual disciplines for the inner regeneration of her racial being. In recent times also she, along with the rest of India, has tried to relive those ancient experiences so as to be ready for a higher destiny. The early attempt of the Brahmo Samaj movement was predominantly Vedantic, though not without a Tantric leaning. Keshab's Vaishnavic heart burst into kirtans; and he was more expressly a worshipper of the Mother. The Sri Ramakrishna movement established the oneness of religious experiences; but the soul of it was a child of the Mother; and Vivekananda sought to apply Vedanta to the practical problems of life. Through her political endeavours the country adored the Mother again. In his philosophical *outlook and in the prose* writings through which he expressed it, Tagore evinced the Vedantic bent of his mind; although his poetry is pervaded with the sweetness and fervour of a Vaishnavic heart. The art of Bengal mirrors her soul's mystic perception of the beauty and wonders of the world of the Spirit, the intangible grace and glory of the gods and goddesses. Thus the cultures of Vedanta, Tantra and Vaishnavism, of knowledge, will and devotion, have flowed in a single stream, as it were, in order to fertilise the mind, soul and heart of India. And every modern movement worth the name has directly or indirectly been nourished by one or all of these streams. It is to be remarked that a very significant feature of all these movements is a constant insistence on the acceptance of Life and its values and a definite discouragement of the otherworldly attitude. They also try to show the fundamental unity of all religions and their chief concern is the truth of the Spirit and never the externals by which religions are known to-day.

This is the beginning, however faint and inchoate, of a new era of spiritual seeking. And Bengal must come out of her present welter of uncertain tendencies and prepare herself for it.

The way to the supreme Perfection that is to come to man in the future lies in a completer synthesis of all the spiritual experiences of the race which so far have separately or in imperfect combinations helped forward its progress towards the goal. But man, as he is to-day, is not the last word of his terrestrial existence. He has a higher destiny to fulfil, a greater life to attain. And this he will do, this godlike Life will be his, through the divinisation of his mind, life and body, to be brought about by an integral spiritual self-culture, and by the answering descent into him of a new Light from above. The Vedic mystics had glimpses of this higher Light. Sri Aurobindo to-day sees it in all its supernal plenitude. He sees it descending on the earth to effectuate the inevitable change in her consciousness. It is that creative power of God—called by Sri Aurobindo the Supermind—which is decreed to be active in the earth and evolve out of man the Superman, even as man has evolved out of the animal. Man, as he rises into this consciousness will change into the gnostic being who will live in Harmony, Peace and Unity for ever and for ever. These gnostic beings will form a perfect spiritual community. Sri Aurobindo says that conditions in earth-nature are tending towards this consummation. He, therefore, calls upon humanity, re-echoing the ancient *rik*:

> "Arise, O Souls, arise! Strength has come,
> Darkness has passed away—the Light is arriving!'

This is a call to the largest fellowship in the luminous world of the Spirit, towards which man has been progressing in his evolution, led by the kindly hand of the unseen Guide.

ACKNOWLEDGMENTS

The sources, especially for the medieval period, are most of them in Bengali. and they are numerous. The pages have not, therefore, been burdened with foot-notes. Below is given a list of the authors and writers whose works and articles in various periodicals on the cultural history of Bengal have been consulted.

The writer gratefully acknowledges the help and suggestions he has received from his revered friends in the Sri Aurobindo Asram while revising the essays for publication in book form.

Authors and writers : Abdul Karim, Amulyadhan Vidyabhusan, Ananda K. Coomaraswamy, Asitkumar Haldar, Atalvihari Ghosh, Bankimchandra Chatterji, Benoytosh Bhattacharya, D. R. Bhandarkar, Dineshchandra Sen, Durgachandra Sanyal, Enamul Huq, E. B. Havell, Haraprasad Sastri, H. D. Sankalia, J. Burgess, J. Fergusson, J. C. French, James H. Cousins, J. Samaddar, J. Woodroff, Kalidas Nag, Kaliprasanna Das-Gupta, Kshitimohan Sen, M. Ziauddin, Mukul Dey, Nalinikanto Bhattashali, Nolini Kanta Gupta, Nagendranath Vasu, Nandalal Bose, O. C. Ganguly, Probodchandra Bagchi, Percy Brown, P. C. Paul, Pramathanath Mukhopadhyaya, Rabindranath Tagore, Rameshchandra Mazumdar, Rajanikanto Chakravarty, Ramesh Basu, Rakhaldas Banerji, Radhagovindo Nath, Radhakumud Mukherji, Rejaul Karim, Sister Nivedita, Sri Aurobindo, Stella Kramrisch, S. Jagadiswaran, Saratchandra Das, Swami Jagadiswarananda, Swami Nirvedananda,

Swami Saradananda, Swami, Vivekananda, Tan Yun-Shan, Tomonashchandra Das Gupta, V. C. Smith, Wazed Ali.

Literature : Ballads of East Bengal, *Chaitanya Charitâmrita, Chaitanya Bhâgavat, Kavikankan Chandi, Mangal Kâvya, Vaishnav Padâvali,* old Bengali, Buddhist, Tantric and Sahajiya literatures.